THE PASSIONATE MUSE

To Phil and Nico

THE PASSIONATE MUSE

Exploring Emotion in Stories

Keith Oatley

OXFORD
UNIVERSITY PRESS

OXFORD
UNIVERSITY PRESS

Oxford University Press, Inc., publishes works that further
Oxford University's objective of excellence
in research, scholarship, and education.

Oxford   New York
Auckland   Cape Town   Dar es Salaam   Hong Kong   Karachi
Kuala Lumpur   Madrid   Melbourne   Mexico City   Nairobi
New Delhi   Shanghai   Taipei   Toronto

With offices in
Argentina   Austria   Brazil   Chile   Czech Republic   France   Greece
Guatemala   Hungary   Italy   Japan   Poland   Portugal   Singapore
South Korea   Switzerland   Thailand   Turkey   Ukraine   Vietnam

Published by Oxford University Press, Inc.
198 Madison Avenue, New York, New York 10016
www.oup.com

Oxford is a registered trademark of Oxford University Press

Library of Congress Cataloging-in-Publication Data
Oatley, Keith.
The passionate muse : exploring emotion in stories / Keith Oatley.
p. cm.
Includes bibliographical references and index.
ISBN 978-0-19-976763-2 (hardback : alk. paper)
1. Emotions.   2. Psychology and literature.
3. Literature—Psychology.   I. Title.
BF511.O377 2011
152.4—dc23
2011049782

1 3 5 7 9 8 6 4 2

Printed in the USA
on acid-free paper

CONTENTS

ACKNOWLEDGMENTS

The title of the short story "One Another" was suggested some 30 years ago by Jonathan Miller as the title of a book we were planning to write together. Like some parts of this current book, the one we were going to write all those years ago was to draw inspiration from Goffman's work on the presentation of self to others. It didn't quite make it from conversation onto the page, but I hope Jonathan won't mind that I have used the title we were going to use, then, for the short story I've written for this book.

I would like to thank Jenny Jenkins, my life partner and the principal editor of all my books. Her insights, corrections, and suggestions have been invaluable. I'd like to thank, also, my colleague Maja Djikic, who also read the manuscript and made valuable suggestions.

The research on which this book is based is part of a new field, the psychology of fiction. I'm very grateful to the people who have come to work with me as graduate students, who have worked on the psychology of narrative, and of fiction, and to my thinking about it. Angela Biason, Valentine Cadieux, Maja Djikic, Mitra Gholamain, Allan Eng, Alison Kerr, Laurette Larocque, Jerry Lazare, Raymond Mar, Rebecca Wells-Jopling. Some of these people—Valentine, Maja, Raymond, Rebecca—continue to work with me, and to publish the online magazine on the psychology of fiction: *OnFiction* which you can find at www.onfiction.ca A few passages in this book were originally published by me in *OnFiction*.

My colleagues in the field of the psychology of emotion are many, and I am grateful to them for interactions and input on the topic of emotion. Among them I would especially like to thank Phil Johnson-Laird and Nico Frijda for their friendship and their influence on my thinking.

During the period in which I have been writing this book and thinking about its topics, the following colleagues in the psychology of fiction have been especially influential for me: Marisa Bortolussi, Brian Boyd, Noël Carroll, Gerry Cupchik, Ronnie de Sousa, Peter Dixon, Art Graesser, Melanie Green, Patrick Hogan, Frank Hakemulder, Don Kuiken, David Miall, Mary Beth Oliver, David Olson, Joan Peskin, Jordan Peterson, Willie van Peer, Brian Stock, Ed Tan, Peter Vorderer.

I'd like to give my warm thanks to the editors at Oxford University Press: Catharine Carlin who commissioned the book, Marion Osmun who discussed part of an early draft, and Joan Bossert who became the book's thoughtful and ever-helpful editor.

CREDIT LINES FOR IMAGES:

Page 1
Henstridge, Fred. "90.0726 of the Helsinki-Leningrad train taken at the Helsinki train station", Copyright © 2011 by *Fred Henstridge Photography*. Used with permission.

Page 39
"Woman in White Blouse", Copyright © 2011 by iStockphoto LP. Used with permission.

Page 61
"Staircase in Hotel Seurahuone, Helsinki", Copyright © 2011 by Hotelli Seurahuone Helsinki. Used with permission.

Page 83
"Helsinki Central Railway Station, Carl Edelfelt, Helsinki, Finland", Copyright © 2011 by Dennis@nomadicpinoy.com. Used with permission.

Page 105
Bellotto, Bernardo. "Bridgettine Church and Arsenal", Oil on canvas, 1778, Warsaw. Brygidki Church on the corner of Nalewki St. Further down is the Warsaw Arsenal. On the left, Bielańska St.

Page 127
Rumpled bedclothes: Hannah Oatley.

Page 145
Man holding coffee cup: Keith Oatley.

ONE ANOTHER

PART I

"East meets West at last, and now we must part," said Alex.

Sonya looked at him, raised an eyebrow, pursed her lips in a half smile.

"I'm worried about you," he said. "You said you were lucky to get this position. It's quite high up, but you don't seem that interested."

"It interests me enough," said Sonya.

"I should have tried to get my visa extended," Alex said. "Having me here would steady you."

"Steady?" she said. "You a steadying influence?"

"I'm a good influence for you."

"You know you wouldn't be allowed. Get this arrangement started with the publishers. You can be back here in a snip."

The year was 1988. Alex sat on a couch with Sonya in her apartment in Leningrad. Alex leaned closer to her, moved his arm against hers, snuggling. To one side, in a red plush armchair, Sonya's mother dozed, with her head resting on the armchair's soft back.

The apartment was a very good one in a very good area, in the Liteyniy district. Its large rooms and high ceilings with elegant moldings had been built in the nineteenth century when St Petersburg was rich. It was large enough for both Sonya and her mother to live in comfortably, without interfering with each other. The big sash windows made it bright, and showed off its comfortable furniture and water colors of harbor scenes, together with a reproduction of painting by Alexei Harlamoff, which Alex particularly liked, of a woman reflected in a mirror, intent on reading a book.

Despite their having grown up in different countries, Alex found he could fit in with Sonya, know her thoughts. He could share her mind. He could sit with her, or walk with her, just be with her. Leaving was wrenching. He would miss her, painfully.

"I'll be all right," Sonya said.

"But ..." He shook his head.

"There's something between us that won't be broken. You must get ready."

Sonya smiled at him in a way that let him know that she knew he didn't want to leave. She knew he was feeling anxious, that he would miss her. She rose from the couch, laid one hand on his shoulder, and kissed him warmly on the lips.

"I'll wake Mama," she said. "She won't want you to leave without saying goodbye to her favorite capitalist lackey."

Sonya's father had been a Party official who died of a heart attack six months previously. The Party had favored him, so Sonya was able to travel abroad. She and Alex had met when she spent a year at the London School of Economics. Sonya's mother had been depressed since her husband died, and sometimes she had difficulties breathing. Sonya had angled for her new job in the Ministry of Health because, with her mother's illnesses, she would be able to know what strings to pull, and whom her mother should see.

It would have felt awkward for Alex to stay in the apartment, so he'd taken a room in a hotel. When Sonya went there and they made love, he embraced her eagerly, wanting to make it right between them. She, as usual, was devoted. Completely. By the second time, in that way that had become familiar to him, the lovemaking seemed a duty. He could not understand it. There remained a yearning in him, for that person with whom making love would complete the meeting of minds. Between him and Sonya, it didn't quite happen. She was on the small side, with an elongated face. Was his reluctance merely physical?

Alex was attractive, though he worried that his cheeks were too round. He was 32, on the tall side. His dark brown hair sprang upward from the middle of his head and curved downward into a fringe. He was affectionate, and able to touch a woman on the arm or shoulder in a way that felt to her exactly right. People found his openness appealing, though some who knew him thought that the way he clenched his jaw at anything he didn't like showed a determination that they wouldn't want to confront.

Alex knew he had a pattern with women. It tormented him. He wondered what was wrong with him. First he would admire a woman from afar, then draw near; but then, if he succeeded, his interest would evaporate like a puff of steam. But not with Sonya. Their relationship had grown in a different way. It had grown from friendship. When they were first together they made daring plans for the future, thinking how to get around regulations. Mostly things worked well between them.

Sonya was clever and capable. When she put her mind to something, she did it superbly. Sometimes Alex would feel annoyed because she seemed to lack ambition. She would focus on him in a way he found cloying, a kind of dependency. He liked being the focus of attention, but not in that way. He didn't know what it was. Too much responsibility, perhaps, that a woman was making him the purpose of her life. He would flinch inwardly. But he loved her mind, which was inventive—a mind with which he could engage, a mind full of ideas. And she was companionable. There had never been anyone else with whom he could contemplate a life together. Perhaps he wasn't trying hard enough.

Alex kissed Sonya's mother who had risen from her armchair as he prepared to leave. Sonya opened the front door of the flat. She kissed him goodbye.

·   ·   ·

The plan was simple. Alex was to go to a house on a street off the Liteyniy Prospekt. Beside the house was an alleyway, and in the alleyway was a door. Under a dismal sky, from which fell drops of occasional drizzle, Alex slipped down the alley. If the door was locked, the plan was off. He tried the handle. It moved with his hand, and he pushed the door open. Inside, he turned so that he could bolt the door, top and bottom. He turned again; concrete steps led down to a dank passage that was dimly lit by a single bulb. On his left were empty wooden shelves from which white paint was peeling. On his right was a wall of exposed rough brickwork. He descended the stairs, holding on to a steel pipe that served as a handrail. The passage led to a bare basement room, also lit with a single bulb. In one corner, damp had invaded. Penetrating damp. An untidy stack of folding chairs leaned against a wall. On the opposite side was a desk. He opened its drawer and took out a large grey envelope, two inches thick. He eased his rucksack from his shoulders, rested it on the desk, undid its straps, and put the envelope in.

Across the room was another door. Alex opened it, went up some more stairs, through another door, and found himself in the front hall of a well-appointed house. Doors opened off from the hall, and a carpeted staircase with oak bannisters led up to the next floor. From a room upstairs he heard the sound of a piano, a Chopin Prelude. In a gilt-framed mirror he glimpsed himself: a man wearing a dark-green anorak, carrying a rucksack. What was he doing, here in someone else's house? What if the pianist stopped and came downstairs? His felt his heart in his chest. He took a breath, tried to calm down. He opened the front door, walked outside, closed the door behind him.

A few minutes later, Alex walked across the Liteyniy Bridge and peered over the stone parapet at the brown River Neva as it flowed sluggishly toward the Baltic Sea. He glanced skywards. Still overcast and—wouldn't you know—there was still a light drizzle. He reached the Finland Station 35 minutes before his train was due to leave. It wasn't the Finland Station that Lenin saw when he arrived there in 1917. That building had been torn down, replaced by a grey concrete structure.

At the station, Alex took from his rucksack a smaller envelope than the one he'd just put in. This one was addressed to Sonya. He put it in a mailbox. In the envelope was a small volume of poems by Anna Akhmatova. On the flyleaf he had inscribed in his italic script. "To Sonya, and to the future, with all my love."

Alex walked through the main station building and out toward the platforms. Six tracks ran northwards. In some trees, rooks were cawing, and there was a sudden flapping of wings, as if they had been disturbed. Alex glanced behind him. No one was following. He walked to his left, and then turned right along Platform 1, where the train was not yet in. He pulled open a heavy glass door of the large waiting room. Oppressive concrete pillars dominated the room, which had formica tables and uncomfortable chairs, a row of windows onto the platform, an odor of sour milk. At one end of the room was a buffet with a counter at which stood a baleful woman who wore an apron.

"Mineral water, please," he said.

"With gas?" asked the sad-looking woman.

"With gas."

Alex handed the woman a handful of change that included an exorbitant tip, and took the glass and the bottle to a table. He removed his rucksack, lowered it to the floor and set it between his ankles. The envelope he had picked up contained a manuscript by a prominent dissident. It was said to be damning of Soviet practices. Even now, in the days of Glasnost, it would be as unwelcome to the authorities as *The Gulag Archipelago* had been in its day.

Alex was to bring the manuscript to his friend David who owned a small publishing house at which he had worked for a while. It was David who had the plan to smuggle out the manuscript so that it could be translated and published in the West. David was the dissident's contact in London. Alex's cover story—perfectly true—was that the large publisher for whom he now worked was cooperating with a state publishing house in Leningrad on a joint project for medical books. Alex had gone to finalize the arrangements.

Alex looked round the waiting room and suddenly felt he was in a John Le Carré book. Here he was on a mission, anonymous enough, conversant with the crossing of borders, able to speak serviceable Russian. It was exciting. But the idea didn't work.

He didn't even know who his adversaries were. Mere anonymity didn't do it.

Had you seen Alex there, you might have thought that with his too-long hair, his green anorak and his rucksack, and with his Ecco shoes, he didn't look anonymous at all. At the same time, you may have observed that no one took any notice of him.

The table wasn't steady, so Alex didn't lean on it. He took a half-sip of water and shut his eyes. He had an image of Sonya three hours earlier as he'd sat with her in her apartment. He remembered how he had walked too slowly out through the apartment's doorway, remembered his few steps across the land-ing and his descent of the first stairs, remembered that, before turning the corner of the staircase, he'd glanced back up to where he could see her slight figure as she stood and held ajar her front door. He remembered his mouth being dry. He remembered her face, looking at him, her lips pressed together to pretend a slight irony, but really to make sure she didn't cry.

He opened his eyes: the dreary waiting room and its drab occu-pants reappeared. His forearm rested on the table and his hand grasped his glass of mineral water. His mouth was dry, again. He took a mouthful of water, which he swirled across his palate. He put down the glass, and put his elbows on the table, which rocked and spilled some water.

Before Alex had gone into publishing, he'd been a stockbroker and was successful enough to afford a house in London, in Belsize Park. He'd not felt satisfied with making money in order to make money. Impulsively, he'd given it up. He was one of those people who read a lot, and thought a lot, and liked to talk about what he'd read, and to think out loud about what was on his mind. He liked the bustle of publishing, the authors, the traveling, the cre-ation of books that would be out there in the world, in libraries, and on people's bookshelves. David had been a friend, who was willing to take Alex on when he'd become bored with brokering stocks. They worked well together.

Alex had been working in David's publishing house for eighteen months when David said, "I've been thinking about a new idea." His idea was to stop publishing across a wide range, and to work on single projects, individually.

"There's this woman," said David. "In Amsterdam. She knows everything there is to know about Vermeer. We'd do a book with exquisite reproductions, all 35 of his paintings in historical sequence, each scaled by the same proportion so that you can turn the pages see the whole sweep, uninterrupted."

"You think it will make money?"

"The book will be expensive. Each picture is a piece of theater, a moment of time made eternal, and there's a story, too, behind each one. We'd show how he used the *camera obscura*. Might have that as a pop-up. We'd explain how some paintings went through drafts, which can be seen from X-rays. And there's van Meegeren who did the forgeries."

"I've heard of him. Was it Vermeers that he forged?"

"He did others as well, but he completely got Vermeer. He didn't copy known paintings, but he had the style, the subject matter, the way Vermeer made pigments, and he found a way of aging the pictures. Most of all, he inhabited the way he thought. One of his pictures is so good that some experts said it was the best Vermeer ever did."

"If it was beautiful, isn't that enough? The pattern on the retina, and in the brain."

"Meegeren had been a painter, but didn't hit the success button."

"And she'll write about all this, this woman?"

"The thing is," David was hesitant. "I'll have projects for you, but to make a steady income you'll need to move."

"Another publisher?"

"I'll fix something up. I know just the thing."

David was one of those people who knew people. He arranged for Alex to keep a desk and a bookshelf in his office but to move to a much larger publishing house, on an 80 percent contract. One day a week, he continued to work for David. The new job was all right. In this job, one of Alex's projects was to publish medical books in association with a Russian publisher. This had the right mixture of the exotic and the useful. It allowed him to see Sonya.

Alex didn't know how David conceived the idea of getting hold of the dissident's manuscript and publishing it. He said he had to keep it under his hat. But it would be a real coup. The publicity would be fantastic. When David broached the idea, Alex found it exciting.

"Have you got the balls for it? That's the question."

Many times since, an image of David's skeptical expression had come into Alex's mind. The balls, he thought. He remembered, too, the face he'd made in response: mock disdain.

"If you're the tough guy why don't you do it?" he'd said to David.

"You wanted to work on challenging projects."

The impulse was strong. Alex agreed. Now in this melancholy waiting room it seemed like an escapade. Only a silly schoolboy would do it. Why put himself in this position? Wanting to please David? Here he was carrying an incriminating object. Mad to agree. Even more mad to be going through with it. Should have dumped it in the river, should tell David, when he got back, that he'd been knocked on the head.

Then came another wave of thought: what mattered was Sonya. He thought back to his desperation and loneliness, his longing to be with her, his chasm of emptiness. They'd been together. It was good. It was. Why had those nagging doubts returned?

Was the drizzle letting up? Not sure. Through the windows of the waiting room, he saw carriages of a train backing slowly in, alongside the platform. Some of the waiting people got up and went out toward the train.

Alex fought to push anxious thoughts from his mind. Childish. He was going to do it. He did have the balls. The border in three hours. He could do it. He clenched his jaw. One step at a time. Get to Finland. That's what.

Alex stayed on his chair until all the people who'd left the waiting room had boarded. Then he went himself. No one else got on the train when he did.

Alex found his compartment. His seat was facing forward, opposite a man and a woman who no doubt were married. The wife had one of those matter-of-fact faces, with the patina of middle-age, lined but firm. The husband looked as if he were the subordinate in the relationship. At the end of Alex's seat, next to the sliding compartment door, was a woman in a beige raincoat, wearing a headscarf. The scarf didn't go well, but the raincoat had a fur collar and looked expensive. Not Russian.

"Good evening," he said, in Swedish.

The woman with the headscarf replied in Swedish. The couple nodded. Probably Finnish, returning from Leningrad where they'd been visiting family.

The compartment was neither very clean nor very dirty, neither recently renovated, nor too old, neither comfortable nor uncomfortable. On the outside of the window were grey vertical streaks and spots of drizzle. Inside there was a smear along the lower edge. This was the little room in which he would sit for six hours.

He took from the pocket of his anorak a copy of *Anna Karenina*, which he placed on the seat beside him. He was working on his Russian, trying to improve. He lifted his rucksack up onto the luggage rack, and put his anorak untidily on top of it. He sat down and stared through the window. He resisted the temptation to get up and stand in the corridor on the platform side, from where he could see if anyone boarded the train at the last minute.

At last, there was movement. The train lurched, as if the driver had gone into reverse by mistake. Then, after a long pause, the train edged forward. Alex pressed his right shoulder and the side of his forehead to the window. Bleak blocks of flats slid past. Who would want to live out here, on the Vyborg side of Leningrad? Where Sonya lived would be all right. Or living with Sonya. Whatever was he doing: smuggling!

The track was not well engineered, and the carriage shook from side to side but, now that the train was in motion, Alex felt some relief, countered by the thought that the real danger would be at the border. Suddenly there was a downpour. Horizontal rain streaked the window. The train slowed and the streaks of rain curved downward like the financial graph of a company about to collapse.

The train started to move faster again, and the window against which Alex leaned jogged against his shoulder, jostling like a carelessly rocked cradle so that, suddenly, he found his eyelids heavy and his eyes closed. When he awoke, the day was fading, and the rain had stopped. They were in a forest, not going fast, because this train did not go fast, but it was going.

The middle-aged couple opposite had dozed off. The woman in the beige macintosh and headscarf was reading a hardback book. Nonfiction. He couldn't see the title.

Alex opened his novel. He read that Anna was on a train. She had a novel with her, just as he had. She was disturbed by the rattling of the train, by the other people in the carriage, by the storm that was flinging snow against the windows. Anna began to read, and to think about what she was reading, but she found she didn't want to concentrate on her book. She wanted to live, not vicariously, but for herself. She wanted excitement.

Alex summoned Anna into his imagination but she slipped away because he, too, found he didn't want to read.

Alex looked out of the window: a pile of planks and construction rubbish beside the track, trees extended into the indefiniteness of twilight. He thought about the manuscript in his rucksack. The dissident was a hero. He imagined the book as having at its center a transformative idea, not just about Soviet society, but about society in general. He looked forward to writing a preface that would be thoughtful and thought provoking. He'd start, perhaps, with a description of how he'd picked the manuscript up from a basement in Leningrad. Back in London, he would make a copy of the book, immerse himself in it, discuss it with the translator, go to the library. It would be a hit. A big hit. He imagined David and himself on television. David's project, really. David would be in the forefront, and that was only right, but still it would be exciting.

At last the train reached Vyborg. It was dark now, but lights were visible at the border. The train stood, for a long time. Suddenly, in the corridor, there was a stamping of boots, a slamming of doors, shouting. Soldiers appeared carrying guns, 19-year-olds. With a violence that might have broken it off its runners, one pulled open the compartment door, came in and scowled at its occupants. Another man, smaller than the first, and without a gun, followed.

"Passports," he said.

Alex had been right about the couple opposite him. They had Finnish passports. He gave his Swedish passport, and looked into the man's eyes. Nothing. Not a flicker of response. The woman in the headscarf also had a Swedish passport. The compartment door slammed, and there was more stamping and banging as the contingent moved along the carriage. Half an hour later, more stamping. The military detail returned. The man who had collected the passports returned them to the Finnish couple and to the woman with the headscarf. No passport for Alex.

"Come with me," the man said to him.

Alex stood up. Don't look at the luggage rack.

He followed the men out onto a low platform, toward a single-storey wooden building at the side of the track, with a telegraph pole beside it. Arc lights splayed their beams onto the building's roof and into the trees.

A soldier in front of him pushed open the door. As Alex was about to enter he was hit in the back. A flare of pain. He cried out, and quickly swiveled. A solder with compressed lips glared at him. Alex felt like smashing the man's face. But these border guards deserved their reputation. The man had the butt of his rifle poised for a second blow.

Inside the wooden building was a kind of vestibule, not much wider than a corridor. It had a bench along one side.

"Sit."

The pain was bad. Was a kidney ruptured? The top of his pelvis cracked? Blood vessels broken? Alone in the vestibule, he grimaced and felt under his shirt, round to his back. A little blood, not much. After ten minutes the pain subsided somewhat. A soldier appeared, and led him to a bare room with a wooden floor, lit by a single bulb under a conical glass shade that hung from the ceiling. A man in officer's uniform sat at a table, not a rickety table of the kind Alex had sat at in the station waiting room. That kind of thing was for the proletariat. This was solid army issue. The table and chair were the only furniture in the room.

"Alex Eklund."

"Yes."

"You traveled to Leningrad. What was your purpose?"

He spoke English with an American accent.

"I work for a publisher in London. I came to arrange a joint project."

"An elaborate journey for a brief meeting."

The man had a thin face. He was altogether thin. A physically unimpressive man. He must be shrewd. Probably cruel.

"We're forming a partnership," said Alex. "I can show you a letter."

"I know about the letter."

Anything could happen. They had infinite power. He had none. By midnight he could be face down in the mud of the Gulf of Finland. Or had they taken him off the train so that they could search his rucksack?

Sweat was running down Alex's forehead, into his eyebrows. Another rivulet ran down his right cheek. He wanted to wipe it with his sleeve, but he kept very still.

"You are perspiring," said the man. "You don't have a handkerchief."

Alex shrugged, and raised his eyes in pantomime fashion.

"Making faces. The English sense of humor."

"I'm Swedish."

"I have complete discretion, here at the border. Certain offenses will not be tolerated."

Alex made no reply.

"Wait there."

The officer left, and a soldier entered. A bruiser. He stood at the side of the room and stared at Alex. Through a thin wall from another room came the sound of an angry voice on the phone, shouting. Alex caught a word or two, not enough to understand. Was the argument about him? He and the soldier stood for another ten minutes.

The door opened. Another uniformed man entered.

Chapter 1

Enjoyment

Fiction is based on narratives in which characters act on their intentions and encounter vicissitudes. Readers enjoy entering into the lives of characters, following their projects, and coming to empathize with them as their plans progress or meet obstacles. Readers enjoy, too, meeting characters with whom they sympathize, and being reminded of emotional episodes in their own lives.

This book is a hybrid[1] of a short story, "One Another," and a discussion of its psychology and emotions.

I hope you enjoyed part I of the short story, and have started to become interested in Alex and Sonya, that you glimpse something of their desires, and begin to feel for them. Perhaps you might start to like them and, of course, I'd like you to want to turn the pages to see what will happen.

Thousands of stories have started somewhat like this one, with a principal character, a protagonist, who has a desire and a plan, and confronts a difficulty. This kind of opening is, I think, the most conventional part of the story that I've written for this book. I've started the story in this way to show commonalities with a tradition in fiction in which there is a character with a plan, and in which there is some suspense.

One might say that fiction is all about the emotions. That's a bit of an exaggeration, but not much of one. As "One Another" continues, you and I can reflect on questions of why emotions are so central. The questions turn out to be of two main kinds.

The first kind is this: why, in stories, is there such concern for the emotions of characters? And more than that: how is it that so many of these emotions are negative—for instance, anxiety or even outright fear, horror, and anger? You might have noticed that in bookshops and video stores, there is often a classification by the kind of emotion you might expect characters to experience. In a comedy, characters start off in difficulties but they attain happiness. In a romance, characters fall in love. In drama, you expect a conflict in which the characters become angry. In a thriller, characters will suffer fear or even terror. In a horror movie, they see something horrible. In a tragedy, characters experience loss and sadness. It seems easy to understand why one might be drawn to fiction that opens a window to happiness and laughter, and to circumstances in which these can arise. It's also not too difficult to understand why one might be drawn to stories of love, because we humans seem often to experience a yearning that romantic stories are designed to resonate with. However, if in ordinary life we were told we would encounter people affected by terrible fear or disabling loss, we might wonder about becoming involved. Yet in a book or a movie, we seem to take pleasure even in the most negative emotions. How can this be?

The second kind of question is this: How is it that the principal emotions of fiction are not those of the characters, but of readers and audience members? Many articles and chapters of books have been written about Hamlet's vengefulness and depression, about Emma Bovary being swept up into a love affair, about Anna Karenina[2] at the end of her story declining into a sad despair. Really, in fiction, however, such character emotions are promptings to our own emotions. We read and watch fiction because we want to be moved by it. If we didn't experience emotions in ourselves, even negative emotions, we wouldn't go to the play, or watch the film, or read the book. Although the emotions of fiction seem to happen to characters in a story, really, all the important emotions happen to us as we read or watch. Opening out from this issue is the question of why we enjoy experiencing emotions.

In the psychological chapters of this book, which include research that's been done over the last 30 years or so, I offer answers, which I hope you'll find satisfying, to the questions about why emotions are so important to fiction.

CHARACTER

We pay money for fiction, we look forward to reading the next paragraph, we sit still for two hours in the theater, we gaze at the television. These activities could seem odd because they generally mean that we've become involved with one or more fictional characters we don't know, who don't even exist. Yet many of us spend a great deal of time with fiction. Curling up in bed to read a novel, going to the movies, watching television dramas, are enjoyable activities. They seem as valuable as many of the other things we do that have more apparently practical purposes.

Character is central to fiction. In ordinary life, we pursue projects of trying to do well in our job, of finding someone to marry, and so on. We enter relationships in which we play the part of ourselves, or a part in which we present ourselves to others in a certain way. In fiction, selfhood takes a new form. We put aside our immediate relationships and concerns and can take on something of the selfhood of an imaginary character. This is called identification.

When you start to read "One Another," you may start to identify with Alex because, as the writer, I've indicated that one of his plans is to smuggle a manuscript out of the Soviet Union and back to London. My hope is that you come to feel sufficiently identified with him that you, too, take on this purpose, in that you want him to succeed. You don't want him to be arrested. You may feel mental pain when he is hit in the back with a rifle butt.

The idea of character has been sneered at by some postmodernist theorists,[3] but it remains the center of fiction for good reason. We humans are, by far, the most social of all the vertebrate animals. We can think of animals in terms of the kinds of lives they live. Sheep live in flocks, eat grass, and, in a sheeplike way, they all tend to do the same thing at the same time. Beavers fell trees with their teeth and make dams that block streams so that they flood into lakes. What do humans do? We humans cooperate in joint projects that we can't do alone. Human life is based on our ability to do this. Even something seemingly solitary like reading a book depends on cooperation between a writer, a publisher, a printer, a bookseller. Human societies and human lives are based on relationships with others, and relationships are based on emotions. We tend to fall in love, to be devoted to our children, to trust some of our colleagues, to hope that something we buy will be satisfactory, to feel angry with those who frustrate or demean us.

Human life is social life. We are taken up in our social relationships. To conduct these relationships our brains are specialized to construct what psychologists call mental models of others. These models are our understandings of the people we know, of their quirks, of what we like and dislike about them. We use this same model-making ability to understand our own selves.

Fiction is enjoyable. By this, I mean it's capable of engaging us. When we say we enjoyed our vacation, we don't mean we spent the whole time eating ice cream or gazing at sunsets (though these might have been included). We mean we were engaged in what we were doing and that we were doing it for its own sake. Fiction offers us this same possibility. It derives from the play of childhood, which was also done for its own sake, and which was also about emotions and relations with others.

Fiction is also useful. It helps us improve our mental models of others and ourselves. Such improvement is a good thing because our mental models are sometimes mistaken and always incomplete.

Fiction is best thought of not so much as something that has been made up, but as a set of narratives about selves and their projects in the social world. It's based on mental models. It's by means of such models that we can explore and understand our own social world. A character in fiction is an imaginary being for whom we are given a model in words. In "One Another," Alex is 32. He dresses unfashionably, and he has a tendency to be impulsive. He is trying to smuggle a document out of the Soviet Union, and he is in an inner conflict about Sonya whom he loves, but to whom he does not feel sexually attracted in the way he feels is essential to a life-long relationship.

One reason we enjoy fictional character, I think, is because fiction enables us to understand character more quickly, and sometimes more completely, than we can understand it in people we meet in ordinary life. Not only that but, in fiction, we can imagine what it might be like to be a certain kind of character, with a certain kind of desire, in a certain kind of circumstance, even when this character isn't the kind of person we are, or the circumstance isn't one we would ever be in.

This idea of character was taken up in English novels of the eighteenth century. The popularity of the novel, a relatively new form at that time, writes the historian Lynn Hunt, "depends on a biologically based ability to understand the subjectivity of other people and to be able to imagine that their inner experiences are like one's own."[4] Reading these novels, 250 years ago, Hunt continues, created a sense of "empathy through passionate involvement in the narrative." Here is an example from a famous novel published in 1740, *Pamela*, by Samuel Richardson.

> ... he kissed me two or three times, as if he would have eaten me.—At last I burst from him, and was getting out of the Summer-house; but he held me back, and shut the Door.
>
> I would have given my Life for a Farthing. And he said, I'll do you no Harm, *Pamela;* don't be afraid of me. I said I won't stay! You won't, Hussy! Said he. Do you know who you speak to? I lost all Fear, and all Respect, and said Yes, I do Sir, too well!—Well may I forget that I am your Servant, when you forget what belongs to a Master.
>
> I sobb'd and cry'd most sadly. What a foolish Hussy you are! said he: Have I done you any Harm?—Yes, Sir, said I, the greatest Harm in the World: You have taught me to forget myself, and what belongs to me (p. 23).

Pamela is sometimes thought of as the first proper novel in English and—along with other novels in a similar vein—it was read widely and with tremendous enthusiasm. Novels were eagerly discussed by a public that took to this form of fiction at a growing rate.

Through novels, readers came to enter into the emotions of others, even others like Pamela the servant girl who, for most readers, would be quite different from themselves. Hunt cites the Enlightenment encyclopedist, Denis Diderot, as saying, of Richardson's narrative: "In the space of a few hours I went through a great number of situations which the longest life can hardly offer across its entire duration."

In writing "One Another," I conceived the idea for the character, Alex, from a chance meeting with a journalist who was half Swedish, whom my partner and I met when we were traveling from Helsinki to Paris. We had taken the train from St Petersburg—the train that Alex took from Leningrad as St Petersburg was called in 1988—and we were due to fly home from Helsinki. However, flights were grounded because of a giant ash cloud that hovered over Europe. We took ferries and trains to Paris, since it seemed nearer the edge of the ash cloud, and we thought it might be easier to get home to Canada from there.

I really liked this journalist, and we talked a good deal on the train. We spent just a few hours together, and although I got to know something of his life and the way he thought, I could not in that time have come to know him deeply. When I started to write my story for this book, I took his appearance—as well as I could remember it—and started up my imagination. At first I gave my protagonist in the story the name of the journalist. Then, prompted I suppose by my train journey from St Petersburg to Helsinki, I started to imagine the project of smuggling a manuscript out of the USSR, and a relationship with Sonya. The idea of smuggling and the idea of Sonya, living with her mother in her apartment, were utterly different from anything in the life of the person I had met. I changed my protagonist's name to Alex. If I have done my job well, you as readers start to become concerned about Alex's emotions, his anxiety as he takes on his project, his worries about his relationship with Sonya.

So why should we become attached to people we don't know, imaginary characters, and start to be concerned with their lives?

An informative experiment—the best I know on this question—was done by Tom Trabasso and Jennifer Chung. They asked 20 people to watch *Vertigo* and *Blade Runner*.[5] Each film has a main character, a male protagonist, whom the viewers come to like, and each has an antagonist who is working against him. Trabasso and Chung stopped each film in 12 places, and at each place they asked the viewers some questions. They divided the viewers into two groups, each of which had to answer different questions. Each time the film stopped, one group of viewers was asked to say how well the protagonist was doing in his plans and how well the antagonist was doing. And, each time the film was stopped, members of the other group were asked about the emotions they themselves were feeling. The results were that when the protagonist was doing well (as judged by the group whose job it was to say how the characters were doing in their plans) the group whose job it was to say how they, themselves were feeling felt positive emotions, happiness, pleasure, relief, and so on. When the protagonist's plans were seen to be going badly, the group whose job it was to say how they were feeling felt negative emotions: anxiety, anger, frustration, and so on. Also, at stopping points when the antagonist's plans were going well (as reported by the group whose job it was to make these judgments), those who were asked to report their feelings felt negative emotions; when the antagonist's plans suffered setbacks, those who reported their own feelings felt pleased.

So when a liked protagonist succeeds in a project, viewers tend to experience positive emotions. When a protagonist is frustrated by another character or by events, viewers are made angry, sad, or anxious. The same goes for reading novels and short stories. Indeed, this phenomenon is so basic that it works for sports as well. When our team or an athlete we like does well, we feel pleased. When the team or the athlete is not doing well, we feel anxious or frustrated. When the character, or the team, or the athlete, succeeds after overcoming difficulties, we feel pleased.

This process offers us a glimpse of how social we are. In it, we see something of our ability to take on the desires of individuals we like and of group projects with which we feel identified. In doing this, we join in something beyond our own egoistic purposes.

A number of writers, especially those who write for film, have proposed that this process is the very spine of a story. A story is about a character who has a desire, which he or she tries to follow. As the character starts to take actions to follow the desire, outcome never matches expectation. Although, in ordinary life, many of our plans work out quite well, an essence of stories—which makes them interesting to us—is that they are studies of how plans don't work out. Usually they don't work out because of something, or more usually someone, who opposes the protagonist's desire. Then, frustrated in each step in the plan, the protagonist's desire increases and effort is renewed. So stories are like sailing boats tacking into the wind. They are zig-zags. First a protagonist zigs toward an object of desire, then a countervailing force, usually personified as an antagonist, causes a zag with the protagonist being pushed away from the goal. Then he or she renews the desire, and zigs again toward the goal. Then there are more frustrations, more renewals of desire against the opposing forces.

Jerome Bruner has said that narrative is about intentions and their vicissitudes. A story is a trajectory of desire, first moving forward, then being frustrated in response to vicissitudes, then with the desire being redoubled. Perhaps the reason we attend so closely to the screen at a good movie or become lost in a book is that we human beings recognize in ourselves the kinds of desires portrayed in fiction. We are creatures of desire, so the desires and intentions of story characters resonate in us.

When we read fiction, we are constantly considering in our own minds the range of characters' next possibilities of action, both physical and mental. In this way, what characters do becomes recognizable within ourselves, although, because the writer has thought long and hard about the story, he or she has often imagined the character into actions that can be surprising. The writer's idea is for these actions to be both surprising and satisfyingly right.

In writing "One Another," I imagined Russian dissident writers whom I admire, like Alexander Solzhenitsyn and Joseph Brodsky.[6] I imagined a manuscript being written that would be uncomfortable to the Soviet authorities. I imagined playing a part in getting the manuscript published in the West, and, although in ordinary life, I would not be able to do what Alex did—to set out to smuggle the manuscript out of the USSR—in the story world, I can take on his desire and his plan, imagine a version of myself on that train, imagine myself hurt by a border guard. I hope you can imagine that, too.

Many of the emotions we experience in stories are of being involved with the story's characters. This happens in four main ways, as I'll explain in the next sections.

EMPATHY

The process of imagining oneself into the life of a character and going along with his or her actions—identifying with that character—is very emotional. It derives from a process about which there is currently a great deal of discussion. The process is called empathy,[7] which means feeling an emotion that is similar to that of someone else. Empathy used to be contained within the concept of sympathy, which, in 1759, was discussed by Adam

Smith in his book, *The Theory of Moral Sentiments*. Sentiment meant emotion, and sympathy (in which empathetic emotions were then included) was the chief of the sentiments discussed by Smith. He thought that it was the glue that holds society together. About 100 years ago, the term *empathy* was coined with its modern meaning. As this meaning peeled off from the previous idea of sympathy, the modern, less inclusive, idea of sympathy came to mean being moved by someone's predicament, not necessarily feeling anything similar to how that person feels, but moved, for instance, toward wanting to help the person or toward understanding the person's difficulties. The important moral sentiment that was at the center of Adam Smith's book, the glue that holds society together, might be called, in modern terms, empathy-plus-sympathy.[8]

Empathy is a process by which, when a loved one achieves a desire and is pleased at a success, we feel pleased too. We can even feel empathy for people we don't know, as when we hear or read about them in a natural disaster or war. However, empathy is not always positive. It's also the process by which, when a person becomes angry with us, we tend also to become angry and prepare to enter into a conflict with that person. In a comparable way, when someone is anxious, we often take on the anxiety. In fiction, this basic emotional process of empathetic feeling of emotions that are like those of others has been adapted and put to use. It's the process that Tom Trabasso and Jennifer Chung found as they cleverly separated—so that we could see what was going on—the question of whether a protagonist's plans were succeeding from the question of what emotions were felt by people watching a film.

In fiction, I think, the process has been taken to a place that must have been new when, tens of thousands of years ago, humans invented the idea of telling stories to one another, so that hearers might put aside their own desires and plans and take on those of story protagonists. Perhaps, at first, tellers of stories talked about their own deeds: anecdotes. Later, storytellers may have told of ancestors and other people who lived in former times. Still later, perhaps, stories came to be of people who were entirely imaginary, who could stand in for the listeners, and represent them.

When we read, we often go to a quiet and comfortable place, and put aside our day-to-day plans and projects. It's a bit like meditation or mindfulness practice, in which, by concentrating on something like one's breathing, one can let go of day-to-day concerns. As we become involved in a piece of fiction, we let go of our own concerns and allow the desires and projects of a story character to take us over. In "One Another" the desires of Alex and his plan to smuggle a manuscript out of the Soviet Union can become our own. Alex is young, and has an open temperament. Two other characters, Sonya and her mother, like him. So we readers tend to like him too. We want him to succeed, but his plan has its perils. At any moment he might be arrested. In my role as writer, I let you know that Alex glances behind himself as he makes his way across the bridge toward Leningrad's Finland Station. You know he's anxious. In the first part of the story, you tend to feel pleased when Alex accomplishes some steps in his plan, when he picks up the manuscript from a dingy basement, when he boards the train, when he finds himself sitting with fellow passengers who seem recognizable and are, therefore, reassuring.

Then Alex is taken off the train by border guards. They are clear antagonists. Their desires run counter to those of Alex-the-protagonist. He is nervous, and he's right to be so. He's hit in the back with a rifle butt. We feel the shock of the blow, a mental version of his pain.

When, as a writer, I started to experience something of what Alex was like, at the very same time I realized he was starting to take on a life of his own, related to the emotions he was experiencing. It turns out that writers quite frequently have some of the same experience as readers do with characters. We find that the characters start to do things that are appropriate to who they are and to the situation they are in, but without us writers having—as it were—to pull the strings. Marjorie Taylor and her colleagues did a study based on interviews with 50 fiction writers to explore this. The writers ranged from professional writers to people who had not yet published anything. All but four reported some experience of characters becoming autonomous in this way. Writers who had published their work had more frequent and more detailed reports of the phenomenon. As compared with the normal population, writers were also more likely to have had imaginary friends as children, and they also scored higher on tests of empathy.

Maja Djikic, Jordan Peterson, and I found a comparable phenomenon in 52 interviews from *Paris Review* with very distinguished writers, including 14 Nobel-Prize winners. In these published interviews, we found that 30 of the 33 writers who were asked a question about whether they made new discoveries in the course of writing said that they did, and most often these discoveries included characters behaving in ways the writers had not expected.

The experience of literary characters becoming independent of the writers who have created them was discussed by E.M. Forster in *Aspects of the Novel*, one of the very best books I know on the psychology of fiction.

The characters arrive when evoked, but full of the spirit of mutiny. For they have these numerous parallels with people

like ourselves, they try to live their own lives and are conse-
quently often engaged in treason against the main scheme
of the book. They "run away," they "get out of hand": they
are creations inside of a creation, and often inharmonious
toward it; if they are given complete freedom they kick the
book to pieces, and if they are kept too sternly in check, they
revenge themselves by dying, and destroy it by intestinal
decay (p. 64).

Alex didn't try to kick the story to pieces, but he did start to
assert himself. As Valentine Cadieux has explained, characters
whom we writers create are probably unacknowledged aspects of
ourselves. At least they draw on aspects of the selves we writers don't develop in ordinary life. For instance, Alex is somewhat
impulsive, a bit bored with his life. That, perhaps, is part of the
reason why the idea of smuggling a book manuscript out of the
USSR appealed to him. In my life, however, I'm fairly content and
not impulsive. I'm probably rather too careful, and if someone
like David in this story were to ask me if I had the balls to smuggle a manuscript out of a totalitarian country, I'd say, "Certainly
not." So Alex allows me to explore an aspect of action that is more
daring than I dare to be, which I wouldn't allow myself in ordinary life.

In a similar way, as readers, we can enter into the lives of
characters who do things we can recognize and go along with but
wouldn't do in our day-to-day lives.

So, as both writers and readers, we imagine ourselves into the
minds of characters as we take on their desires and plans. The circumstances of the story tend to take precedence over other influ-
ences in how the writer imagines the character. In psychology
there is a principle that helps to explain this effect. It is called
the actor-observer bias.[9] This bias, in ordinary life, means that

we tend to experience what we ourselves do and what others do in rather different ways. If I am a student and I work long into the night for weeks studying for an exam, I might experience myself as studying hard because I know the exam will be difficult and I know the result will be important for my future. If I were to see another student working long into the night for weeks studying for an exam, I might say she was conscientious or ambitious. When we act, we tend to see ourselves as being responsive to circumstances, and doing what is necessary to pursue a plan. When we see others doing exactly the same thing, we tend to attribute their actions to some persisting aspect of their personality. It's rather like when you're driving and have to brake suddenly to avoid hitting that careless person in front.

When we enter a story world of fiction, we start to see the protagonist as responsive to circumstances, that is to say, as more like the way in which we experience ourselves than the way in which we typically see others in everyday life.

As writers or readers, we feel the kinds of emotions the character would feel in following a plan and entering the situations that result, but as writers and readers, we don't feel the character's emotions. We feel something that is perhaps similar to those emotions, but they are not the character's. They are our own. That's how empathy and identification work in fiction.

SYMPATHY

Although we can enter empathetically into the experience of a character, we might imagine a scale of personal involvement with literary characters. At one end of the scale is empathy, in which we can almost become the character. Toward the other end of the scale, we are more distant. We are spectators, and we view the character's circumstances a bit more from the outside. Perhaps we don't yet know much about the character. The kind of emotional state we might then feel is sympathy. We don't become like the character, but we can come to feel for them in their predicament. This is what happens in the first part of "One Another" when we read about Sonya. We know something of her situation, but at the beginning of the story, we don't yet know much about her.

T. S. Eliot described the process whereby, in fiction, a reader feels a sympathetic emotion. It's based, he said, on an "objective correlative." For the reader to experience an emotion—he said—the writer must describe an objective pattern (the "correlative") of external circumstances or events in the world of the story. The pattern of these events, then, is a correlate of a particular emotion. If, for instance, the pattern is of a danger, the emotion is fear. The most widely accepted psychological theory of emotions, known as appraisal theory,[10] makes a similar proposal. The theory of appraisal is, however, better than that of the objective correlative because it's not just about the external world. It's of the relation between external events and a person's concerns or plans. A particular kind of emotion—so this theory proposes—is caused in a character by a particular concern being affected by a pattern of events that impinge on this concern. If a character has a loved one (about whom he or she is concerned), and the event is that this person is lost, the character tends to feel sad. If a character has a plan that he or she regards as important, and the pattern of external events is the frustration of this plan by another, the character tends to feel angry.

In literary terms, as readers we can understand such configurations of concerns and events, and know how each kind of event would strike the character it affects. Thereby, we know the emotion the character would be likely to feel, and we can also feel sympathy for that character in his or her predicament.

So, as well as the process by which we identify with a character by means of empathy we can also feel sympathy for characters based on our understandings of the patterns of concern-related events that authors depict.

In practice, there may not always be much to separate empathy from sympathy. I think the question is really about focus, the way an author presents different characters, whether they are primary or secondary, whether we are near the beginning or end of a story, how well we have got to know these characters, how close we feel to them. We can move back and forth between empathy and sympathy. At the beginning of "One Another," it seems to me we are likely to feel empathy for Alex, and sympathy for Sonya whose father has recently died, who lives with a depressed mother. For Sonya, we know her loved one, Alex, is fond of her, but we wonder how far she is aware of his inner struggles about desiring her sexually.

Edward Royzman and Paul Rozin have found that when we don't know someone very well, as we don't know a character at the beginning of a story, we find it easier to feel sympathy if he or she is in difficulties. We have to know a person or a character quite well before we start to sympathize with them in their successes. Over many years, and with the writing and reading of many stories, authors have come to know this principle. So, at the beginning of many stories, a reader's first acquaintance with a protagonist is when he or she is in trouble, and this trouble sets the story going. I've used this principle in "One Another." As we get to know a character better, our sympathy may turn to empathy.

RELIVED EMOTIONS

Empathy and sympathy occur with what have been called fresh emotions, from our relationship with characters and from events that happen to them in a story. But stories can evoke emotions of another kind, from personal memories.

In the research group of which I am a member, one of the methods we use is to give people a printed story and ask them to write an E in the margin when they experience an emotion (a fresh emotion), and an M when they have a memory from their life that the story has triggered (which might include a remembered emotion). After reading, we ask the participants to go back over the Es and Ms to say what the emotions and memories were and, for the memories, to say whether they included any emotions.[11]

In our first study using this method,[12] Angela Biason and I were helped by two English teachers at a large high school, who let us take over their classes for two periods. We gave each student a story to read. It was either Alice Munro's "Red Dress," which has a female protagonist, or Carson McCullers's "Sucker," which has a male protagonist. Both are stories of identity with protagonists in their teens, the same age as the readers. We took it that the more Es and Ms the students marked, the greater was their personal involvement in the story. Male students had many more emotions and memories when they read the story with the male protagonist than when they read the story with the female protagonist. By contrast the female students experienced emotions and memories to the same extent when the stories had either male or female protagonists. We concluded that teenage boys found it easier to relate to someone closer to their own experience, another teenage boy. Girls were able to relate to, and identify with, a protagonist of either sex.[13]

Tom Scheff has argued that stories can evoke emotional memories from our own lives when the emotions involved have not been fully assimilated. The story then prompts us to relive them. We might say that, according to this theory, all the E's that occur when reading a story are really M's. What happens, says Scheff, is that in people's day-to-day lives, although some emotions are fully assimilated, others are not. People might block them out in the way that can occur if they've been hurt in love and say they're never going to have another romantic relationship again, ever. People generally do this by trying to cut themselves off emotionally. Scheff says that, for these people, emotions are overdistanced: they are held away, or suppressed, in an attempt to avoid them. Sometimes, by contrast, people can't assimilate their emotions because they are overwhelming. These emotions are underdistanced.

We can only fully understand and accept our emotions, says Scheff, when they occur at about the right distance. According to Scheff, the function of literary art, as well as practices such as religious rituals, is to enable significant emotions to occur at the right aesthetic distance, a distance at which they can be experienced fully and assimilated.

When people cry at a performance of Shakespeare's *Romeo and Juliet*, says Scheff, it's because they re-experience the emotion of a significant loss at a better aesthetic distance than the one at which it was originally experienced. If, in people's lives, there remain emotions that have never been fully assimilated, fiction can be a means for experiencing them.

UNIVERSAL EMOTIONS

In the West, the foundational text on how fiction works was Aristotle's *Poetics*. The equivalent version in India was the

Natyasastra by Bharata Muni, who lived perhaps 200 years after Aristotle. The central idea about how fiction works for Aristotle and his followers was *mimesis*, the relation of literary art to the world, usually translated as representation or imitation. In Indian poetics the fundamental issues were different. The principal Sanskrit terms were *dhvani*, meaning suggestion, and *rasa*, meaning literary emotion. These terms focus not on the text's relation to the world but on the relation between poet and listener or between actor and audience member in the theater. *Dhvani* (suggestion) was thought to be the soul of poetry. The function of poetry, drama, and other kinds of fiction is to suggest within the context of a *rasa*, an emotion that can be recognized widely in the minds of readers or audience members.

Rasas are like the emotions of everyday life, but unlike them in that they are felt in fiction in a way that can make them more understandable. *Rasas* are, as it were, essences of the everyday emotions that people remember from their lives. Playgoers (and readers) can cultivate their understanding of works of art, in part to achieve experiences of these *rasas* that seem not so much individual, not just their own emotions, but universal: aspects of all humankind.

Rasa theorists argued that there are nine fundamental emotions in ordinary life, called *bhavas*. Corresponding to these is an equivalent set of literary emotions, the *rasas*, as follows:

Bhava	Rasa
sexual delight	the amorous or erotic
laughter	the comic
sorrow	the pitiable or tragic
anger	the furious
perseverance	the heroic
fear	the terrible

disgust or disillusion	the odious or loathsome
wonder	the marvelous
serenity	the peaceful

The first part of "One Another" is based on the *rasa* of the heroic, which corresponds to the everyday emotion of perseverance. Despite his doubts, Alex has to persevere. As readers, we can appreciate this and can, I think, feel for him as he does it.

The *rasa* theorists believed that, in everyday life, we don't always understand our emotions because, as they put it, we can be blinded by a thick crust of egotism. They say that, in a play or other work of literature, we can experience an emotion in *rasa* form by bringing to bear the experience of our past lives. In more modern terms, we might say that we can bring to bear our understanding of our kinship with all humanity, of all the people we have known, of our experience of other dramas we have seen, and other works of literature we have read. Indeed, fiction gives us the opportunity to live many lives.

In Scheff's theory (discussed in the previous section) emotions of fiction are experiences of emotions that are relived at the right aesthetic distance when, in life, they were not fully assimilated because they had been suppressed or because they were overwhelming. But many emotional incidents in our lives are experienced quite fully at the time; we remember them precisely because they were emotional. It was the emotion that signaled the significance of the event to us, made it memorable.

If, during the day, you experience an emotion that you still remember in the evening, on approximately 90 percent of occasions, you will have told it to a friend, a relation, or a loved one. This is an important finding made by Bernard Rimé. If you've ever wondered, after telling in confidence an emotional incident to someone else, whether that person will pass it on, you can stop wondering. If the incident has prompted an emotion in the person you have shared it with, there's a 90 percent chance they will have told it to someone else.

Emotions are shared because they are the compass-readings of our lives. In sharing an emotion, implicitly I ask myself and the person with whom I'm sharing it: what's the direction to which this emotion is pointing? What does it mean about me? Does this way in which I felt mean I'm feeling things in the right way? Did I act properly? Did other people in the incident behave well? When I talk with others about my emotions, I ask what they would have felt. What would this kind of event have meant to them?

Emotions are evaluations of events as they affect our concerns, and in discussing them we enlarge our experience of them. The idea of *rasas* extends this concept. A *rasa* experienced in a story is based on a kind of emotion that we have experienced, and a story then gives us an opportunity to experience it in a new context, in a way that expands our understanding.

We can think of *rasa* theory as drawing on the remembrance of things past,[14] on emotional incidents from our life that are remembered because they were significant. Stories can be designed to give cues that will evoke memories of such incidents: successes, losses, strivings, frustrations, and so on. Generally, therefore, we can say that one of the ways in which we experience emotions in literature is when the writer sets off an emotional memory.

An everyday emotion is tied to our own concerns, which sometimes can be quite petty. The idea of *rasa* is wider, to make possible a realization that the emotion we are feeling is an aspect of humanity. *Rasas* can be thought of as traces in people's minds, which writers and actors strive to activate by two means: literary characters and circumstances. Together these means are intended not only to prompt an experience but also to encourage a state of reflection on it.

WAYS OF SUGGESTION

The four methods described above, by which emotions can be evoked in readers of stories—the fresh emotions of empathy and sympathy, the remembered emotions of relived incidents, and universal *rasas*—were proposed separately, each as an explanation of how emotions can occur in literature. But they are not exclusive. They are better thought of as four methods by which a writer can suggest, and a reader or audience member can experience, emotions in stories. In reading a novel or short story, we might feel an emotion prompted in one way, then an emotion prompted in another way. Writers can use all these methods in a story. Although some methods—for instance the encouragement of identification with a character who will then be put in danger—prompt in the reader a rather specific kind of emotion, in this case anxiety, for the most part the author would much sooner you, the reader, would enter the story in something like the role of the character, follow the actions and events, and then experience your own emotions in your own way.

PART II

The uniformed man handed Alex his passport and marched him back to the train. The Finnish couple and the Swedish woman were in their seats, as he'd left them.

Alex sat down heavily, resisted the impulse to let out a sigh. The pain in his back was still bad. His heart was still pounding horribly. He glanced at his rucksack on the luggage rack. It was there, with his anorak on top of it, untidy, where he'd left it.

Almost immediately after Alex sat down, as if it had been waiting for him, the train started to move. Then it stopped, waited, then started again. Finally it started to move with deliberation. No lights were now visible, they were in the vastness of the northern forest. They were in Finland. Alex stared out of the window but saw only reflections of the compartment.

The interior of the compartment was hot, as if the heating had been switched on because, in Finland, people needed to be kept warm. Alex turned from the window. He looked at the married couple, who were sitting quietly opposite him. Were they disapproving? Did they think he was a criminal? Were they angry that he'd held up the train? The wife met his eyes and gave him a shy smile.

"They like us to know who's in charge," said the husband in perfect Swedish. He was balding. He raised his eyes as if in surprise with the effect that his forehead wrinkled into a field of parallel furrows.

"Very much in charge," said Alex. He wanted to gush about what had happened: the rifle butt, the senseless interrogation, the shouting.

Alex turned to the woman sitting to the left of him. She had taken off her headscarf and her coat. Without her scarf she looked younger. She was about 30, with good bone structure, and straw-colored hair. She turned toward him and smiled, a friendly smile. Her nose was bent slightly to one side, as if she had been a boxer and her nose had been broken by a punch. Instead of it being disfiguring, it looked extraordinarily attractive.

Relief suddenly enveloped him like the water of a hot bath. Suddenly the compartment was a cozy room in a friendly house, among friends whom he'd known for a long time. He smiled in turn at each of them. It seemed as if they might all burst out laughing.

He couldn't help glancing to his left again. The 30-year-old woman was still looking at him. She smiled again, a smile that was warm, intimate. Was this just the friendliness of two Swedish people having crossed a border from Russia into Finland? Or was it something else?

Alex looked at his knees, then looked toward her again. She was still looking at him. He had sat six feet away from her for three hours, and had barely noticed her. Suddenly she was of extraordinary interest. Who was she? A business woman, from Stockholm? An academic perhaps?

He didn't look at her. He wanted to study her carefully, without her noticing. He waited long enough for the train to make some progress. When he looked again she was reading. In profile, her nose did not look displaced. It was of Roman shape. She sat upright, poised, confident. Her neck seemed unusually long. She wore a tailored white blouse which, from where he was sitting, displayed the profile of a perfect breast, so fascinating that it made it difficult for him to stop thinking about it.

Who was she? She wore black traveling shoes, sensible but expensive, and a grey fitted skirt. Her stockings were sheer, not the kind one would buy in Russia. Perhaps her father was a well-established surgeon, he thought, and her mother a pianist of note. Although she was young, she was already a respected historian who had traveled from Stockholm to Leningrad to consult an archive. She was reading the recently published book of a colleague whose work she admired. She lived in a modern flat, in central Stockholm. She'd recently broken up with a rather inadequate fellow who was obsessional and self-absorbed, who had not been able to appreciate her or to care for her properly...

Chapter 2

The Suspense of Plot

To understand a character's actions in a story, we want to know how things will turn out. We are held in an enjoyable suspense, which is a main purpose of plot. Tension builds, lasts over time, and heightens the reader's relief when a plan is accomplished.

In Chapter 1, I discussed how fiction is enjoyable because of our fascination with the character of others and the character of ourselves. A second reason for enjoyment is plot, an idea that—like that of character—has been sneered at by some critics.[1] But plot is central. It's about human action and human vulnerability.

In day-to-day life we're very interested in how actions turn out. To think about our lives is to think of them as narratives of intentions and actions, including accidents of birth and circumstance, of meetings with others, of achievements, of situations we did and didn't foresee. Stories are about intentions and actions: reasons for the intentions, effects of the actions.

Another way of considering plot is by thinking that drama has a core of conflict, protagonist against antagonist. In "One Another" Alex acts against the Soviet authorities. Drama can also be about other forces. A protagonist may be pitted against a world that can't be fully comprehended, or against unconscious and unintentional aspects of the self. This also happens for Alex. He tries to exert himself against forces within him that are partly unconscious. They militate against his more deliberate intention to commit himself fully to Sonya.

ACTION

In *Poetics*, the foundational discussion of narrative fiction in the West, Aristotle described plot as the structure of actions, and said it was the most important aspect of tragedy. We can generalize: plot is important to all stories. Although postmodernist literature may minimize it, a story without the actions of a plot is generally not much of a story.

The first thing to say about a plot is that it unfolds in a sequence of events. One event causes another. The center of story-plots is that we humans insert ourselves into such chains of cause and effect. We act in the hope of making something happen: something physical, something mental. As compared with mere movement, action always has an element of the voluntary, prompted by an intention to accomplish something. Putting this another way, we act for reasons. Plot is the literary version.

In ancient stories there were characters called gods. The difference between us and them was typically depicted in terms of humans being mortal as compared with gods who were immortal. Although human mortality is not nugatory, it's just a fragment of human vulnerability. So, in the *Iliad*, the human parts of the story are of conflict, uncertainty, and muddle. By comparison, Homer says that the *Iliad's* events occurred because of the will of Jove, a god. There's no vulnerability here. Jove willed it, and that's what happened. If we humans could act with full knowledge of outcomes, peace would reign in the world, there would be no divorce, bridges would never collapse, and executive officers of companies would never have to lie. One may wonder whether stories came into the world as ways of reflecting on our vulnerability.

Narrative fiction is a principal way of exploring, further than we otherwise might, how we should understand ourselves and each other in a world of uncertainty, too complex ever fully to understand. In "One Another" should Alex have put himself in danger by trying to smuggle a document out of the Soviet Union? Should he stop vacillating and commit himself to Sonya, or keep searching, perhaps, for that perfect someone?

NARRATIVES AND SCRIPTS

As I mentioned in chapter 1, Jerome Bruner said that narrative—he might equally well have said plot—is about intentions to make something happen, and the vicissitudes these intentions meet. Such vicissitudes—obstacles, impediments—occur because humans are not all-powerful. Most frequently, they derive from conflict with others who also want to insert themselves into chains of cause and effect. In addition, some of the most subtle stories are about conflicts within ourselves.

Bruner said, too, that narrative—about ourselves as agents with plans and expectations—is a basic form of human thinking. It can be contrasted with the form of thinking we use when we are trying to understand how something physical works, like the weather, or why our geraniums aren't growing properly.[2] Narrative plot is central to fiction because fiction is fundamentally about human intentions, about understanding selves and others in the social world. By contrast, the usual mode of thinking and writing about how things work in the physical and biological world is explanation.

In psychology there is an important idea that in some ways is equivalent to plot. It's the idea of a script: a series of actions, intended to accomplish some result in a way that follows a recognizable pattern.[3] The best known version of the idea was introduced by Roger Schank and Robert Abelson. They conceived it as part of a project to write computer programs that would understand stories.[4] Their favorite example of a script uses the sequence of going to a restaurant: one feels hungry, enters a restaurant, orders what one wants, receives it, eats it, pays, and leaves. A writer needs only mention the word *restaurant*, or even a single element in the script, and anyone in Western culture will be able to infer the whole sequence. If a writer says: "He sat in Bertorelli's, paid for the meal, but left without taking a mouthful," the reader notices the deviation from the script and attends to it.

Scripts are not just cognitive components of understanding. They can also be sequences that are deeply rooted in a society's beliefs and values. A writer can invoke a script with which the reader can resonate. One such is of heroism. Its sequence includes: leaving the safety of home, going alone on a journey, facing dangers that could mean being killed, bringing back something of value to the community, perhaps knowledge perhaps something physical. I mentioned in chapter 1 that, according to the Indian theory of *rasas*, Alex in part I of "One Another" is taking part in the *rasa* of the heroic. He leaves his day-to-day world, goes on a journey of some danger, is taken to a place where he could be killed, aims to bring back home something of value. The idea of a *rasa*-emotion resonates with the idea a script, and I hope that, in readers, this resonance has something of both apprehension and perseverance.

Heroic journeys recur in mythology, worldwide. This kind of pattern is sometimes called an archetype. In "One Another," I have drawn on it in a low-key way. Alex has left a comfortable home in London, with an idea of seeing his girlfriend, then visits a dank basement, and then sets off in a drizzle from a squalid waiting room at a concrete railway station to cross the border into Finland. Nonetheless the underlying *rasa*-script is the heroic.

One can, as the Indic theorists say, see patterns of this kind as residing as traces in the mind, able to be evoked by a story. Most analyses of emotions, including the idea of appraisal, which I discussed in chapter 1, are about events in relation to concerns. Each invokes a single emotion. The concept of *rasa*-traces amplifies the idea because *rasas* usually extend in time. They are script-like sequences, each based in a series of thematic actions and events, such as the heroic journey. As readers of "One Another," we subconsciously pick up the heroic script, feel concern at the obstacles, and, perhaps, draw on the theme's energy and forward movement, as Alex does when he sees the train for Helsinki backing into the station. At this point, he feels he can accomplish the task he has taken on. We may feel anxious for him, but at the same time we feel a determination for him to succeed in his quest.

LIFE AND ART

Human action is central for us humans because our projects are critical to our lives. These lives involve actions, which we take alone or in collaboration with others or in conflict with others. We are completely concerned with them: whether we should get married, whether we will be able to get a certain job, whether a loved one will accomplish some goal. In fiction, we transfer our interest in the projects of ourselves, our family, and our friends, into an interest in the projects of characters.

It may seem paradoxical, but taking on concerns of fictional characters may be enjoyable because we can't influence what happens. Outcomes aren't up to us, and our day-to-day lives are not affected.[5] Our interest remains strong enough that we do like to turn the pages to see what will happen. Secretly, too, we know that, if authors have done their job properly, things will turn out in ways that will be both surprising and satisfying. Things will happen that we hadn't thought of, implications will be expanded and explained, and there will be a resolution (not necessarily a closed one) that may deepen our understanding.

Plot is well chosen as a center of fiction because, not only does it bring into focus an issue of utmost importance—the nature and consequences of human action and emotions—but because it brings into focus, too, our human propensity to evaluate action and its implications. Should the protagonist act in this way? Isn't it despicable to do what the antagonist did? Although it might sound a bit childish to put it like this, we find ourselves thinking in terms of struggles between right and wrong.

Dolf Zillmann has proposed that people who watch movies and read fictional books are highly concerned with whether characters behave well. He says, for instance, that each person who engages with a drama or comedy is "a moral monitor who applauds or condemns the intentions and actions of characters."[6] In a number of experiments, it has been found that people experience pleasure when a liked character behaves well and succeeds. People experience frustration and anxiety when a disliked character behaves badly and succeeds. If, in a thriller with a confusing plot, you wonder which character is the real baddie, he's the one who acts with contempt to an underling.

We constantly evaluate the goodness and badness of characters' actions. When a good character achieves retribution for a wrong that he or she has suffered, or when a bad character is punished, people are sensitive to the level of revenge or punishment that occurs. We enjoy stories more when this seems appropriate. There is even a name for this: poetic justice.

René Weber and colleagues have put this theory to the test by asking whether people's feelings toward characters in a story and the extent to which characters deserve what happens to them underlie enjoyment of the story. More than 500 women students were asked to evaluate 12 characters in a televised soap opera. The women were not fans of the soap opera, which ran on a television channel every weekday for 10 weeks, and they were not asked to watch the whole series. Each watched, in her own time, just one week's episodes on a DVD she was given. After watching the episodes, each participant made ratings of each character (from extremely moral to extremely immoral), and of outcomes for each character (from extremely good to extremely bad). She then rated the extent to which she found the show enjoyable and entertaining. At the same time, the researchers recorded Nielsen ratings (the television industry's estimate of viewers' numbers) for the show. The findings were that enjoyment of the women in the survey, and the Nielsen ratings, were highest when good outcomes occurred to characters who behaved well and bad outcomes occurred to characters who behaved badly. We can think of this study as a version extended over 10 weeks of the kind of effect found by Trabasso and Chung on viewers who watched two films, discussed in chapter 1.

Part of our pleasure in the social world is our evaluation of the actions of others. We enjoy it in our conversations about people we know. We enjoy it in fiction when we think of the actions of characters.

In "One Another," is it right for Alex to be smuggling? The activity is clearly illegal. Perhaps Alex's smuggling is justified because Soviet society should not have been so repressive. What do you think? And what about Alex's idea that for two people to commit themselves to each other for life there should be an unmistakable erotic spark between them? What do you think? Perhaps you think, yes, of course, Alex should worry about his difficulties in making a commitment, because failing to make a full commitment is often destructive to a relationship. Or perhaps you think he is too concerned for himself and not trying hard enough.

Fiction invites you to think your own thoughts and have your own feelings, but in the circumstances of the story. These circumstances may have some relation to those you face yourself or they may be completely unlike anything you've ever faced. What would you do in these circumstances? How do you feel about this character's actions?

So fiction is about the moral world, but without moralizing. At least it had better not moralize or it will seem clunky. Just as fiction is not about telling us what to feel, it's not about telling us how to act.

SUSPENSE

If plot is about action and if, in the story world, the outcome of action is uncertain, then suspense is the emotional state of curiosity. Curiosity might be thought of as a fifth method of prompting emotions (alongside empathy, sympathy, and the two kinds of emotions of memory discussed in chapter 1). We can be curious even if we neither empathize nor sympathize with a character. William Shakespeare's Richard III is an example. At the beginning of the play that bears his name, the hunchback, Richard, limps onto the stage and says:

Now is the winter of our discontent
Made glorious summer by this son of York.

He explains that because he is so misshapen he cannot take part in the pursuits of love, so he is "determined to prove a villain." He is embittered. We are curious. We look on in fascination, as if watching a cobra, not to see *if* it will strike, but to see *how* it will strike and to what effect.

So, in fiction, we experience not just emotions that are negative, but people who are negative, whom in ordinary life, we would seek to avoid. In fiction, we experience some of these emotions as suspense.

In part I of "One Another," we felt anxiety for Alex, and we may have enjoyed it. There seems to be a paradox, because anxiety is supposed to be negative, but perhaps it isn't. Perhaps emotions are mental states that we not only become caught up in but also that we enjoy being caught up in, even when, in ordinary life, we regard them as very aversive. Perhaps it's not the emotions, as such, but, rather, certain conditions of our lives that are aversive: threats, losses, frustrations, and so on. The emotions themselves—anxiety, sadness, anger—are fascinating. They draw us toward them, take us into themselves.

Perhaps the emotions of fiction are important because they occur in a kind of laboratory. Just as scientists study reactions in a controlled way on a laboratory bench, with more precision and without the implications of doing it for real in the day-to-day world, so we can experience our emotions in fiction in a safe way: a way that we can really get into. Just as an engineer builds a computer model, a simulation, of a bridge and tests out possibilities rather than just putting it up and hoping for the best, so we can enter fictional relationships and situations without the danger that they will devastate us. We can experience emotions—states that tell us about what we value—but without negative consequences of actual events in our actual lives.

In day-to-day life, an emotion evaluates an event, gives it importance, makes it urgent to deal with, makes it welcome or something to avoid or confront. It's the event that's the issue. As Robert Louis Stevenson said in 1884, life imposes itself on us,[7] and severely negative events can wreck our lives. Emotions mediate the urgency of such events. By comparison, in fiction there is no imposition, because we enter a work of fiction only if we wish to. In fiction, the events mediate the emotions.

Perhaps think about it like this: rather than a laboratory or test bench, fiction is a kind of play. Just as children play delightedly with the idea of conflict in games of chase and of rough-and-tumble, so we can experience our own emotions and their implications for relationships in fiction. One might even wonder whether, at some time in the last 200,000 years or so during which humans have used language, the story form emerged to enable us to imagine situations without having just to go blindly into them when they actually occur. It's not so much that the situations of fiction are untrue. It's that, for us, they may not have happened yet.

Noël Carroll has written that "emotions are the cement that keeps audiences connected to…narrative fictions,"[8] and these emotions can even include outright fear and horror. Carroll is a philosopher, and he explains the effect in terms of a difference between belief and thought. Just as I have argued that fiction doesn't tell us how to feel or how to act, it also isn't about what to believe. Giving material for belief is the job of writers of nonfiction. A historian might write that the Soviet Union was dissolved at the end of 1991. That's something to believe. If we don't believe it, we could search for evidence that would give a firm basis for belief about what happened. If fiction writers were to write about what to believe, fiction wouldn't work because some of it is, in a strict sense, unbelievable. We don't believe Alex is someone who exists. We know he is a character in a story. He is a creature of the mind.

So, as Carroll puts it, the job of a writer of fiction is not to suggest beliefs but to suggest thoughts. We might call them imaginations. Many of them are suggested by the writer in such a way as to prompt emotions. As one of his examples of the difference between belief and thought, Carroll says that if we are chopping vegetables and we imagine plunging the knife into our eye, we feel a shudder of horror, even though we don't believe we would ever do such a thing. It's the thought of it that is horrible.

In "One Another," we may have the thought: "Alex could be beaten to a pulp and left face down in the mud of the Gulf of Finland." If we are attached to the character, Alex, we might feel anxious, because his situation with aggressive border guards is dangerous for a person who is doing something illegal. We have read enough in newspapers to know how men can behave when they carry guns. The function of anxiety in this kind of story, says Carroll, is to focus our attention and interest. We search the text for further thoughts about Alex's situation, to see what he might do about his situation and about what might come to pass.

In a narrative, says Carroll, we seek answers to the questions that are raised in the narrative. For Alex, after he has been taken off the train and hurt, one question is: Will he be hurt more? When he is interrogated, our questions include: Do they know he's trying to smuggle a manuscript out of the country? Will the manuscript be discovered? Will Alex be imprisoned? Our sense of satisfaction depends on whether the story achieves closure on the questions it has raised.

Questions are not always asked explicitly in stories, though in some, such as detective stories, they are. For instance, in one of Agatha Christie's most highly regarded detective novels, the question—the only question—is who killed Roger Ackroyd?

However, in every story there are questions as you read, and some readers like to make them explicit for themselves. Why did Alex take on the assignment of smuggling the manuscript? Wasn't there something foolhardy about doing this?

In part II of "One Another," after the suspense of wondering what might happen at the border, readers feel some relief. Alex is back on the train, and it crosses into Finland. His rucksack looks as if it has not been touched. The other people in his compartment can see he has been through an ordeal, and they seem sympathetic.

However, the story hasn't reached closure. Questions remain, of whether Alex will succeed in bringing the manuscript back to London, of whether it will be translated and published, of what its effects might then be.

Some psychologists argue that suspense is the very key to understanding the emotions of fiction, and that suspense itself is enjoyment. Before we pick up a book or turn on the television or go out to a movie, our current mood may not have been bad but it may not have been quite right, or there may have been a question about what to do with some stretch of time—for instance, on a train journey. So we may choose a piece of entertainment in which we will not be bored, or one in which we can put aside a worry about some problem in our life, or one in which we won't ruminate in distress or anger about some event that has happened to us. We know how to choose pieces of fiction that will take us out of ourselves so that we want to turn the page or want to gaze contentedly at the screen and wonder what will happen next.

This sense of being taken out of ourselves has been called transportation. Richard Gerrig, who coined the term, thinks it's at the center of our involvement in fiction. It's as if, in a story, we are transported to another world. It's remarkable that it's not hard to imagine ourselves into the St. Petersburg of 150 years ago, as we do in Fyodor Dostoyevsky's *Crime and Punishment*, or even onto a moon of Alpha Centauri, as we do in James Cameron's *Avatar*.[9]

In a recent experiment, Nurit Tal-Or and Jonathan Cohen had participants watch a clip from Edward Burns's (1995) film *The Brothers McMullen*. These brothers are sons of Irish Catholics in Long Island, New York, and one of them, Jack, becomes interested in a woman friend of his wife. The researchers measured transportation by the degree to which people agreed with such statements as "I was mentally involved in the scenes I was watching," "I would like to know how the movie ends," "The scenes affected me emotionally." Identification was measured by participants' agreement with statements such as "I think I understand Jack well," "While viewing I felt like Jack felt," and "During viewing, I could really 'get inside' Jack's head." The researchers found that transportation and identification were different. Transportation had mainly to do with the plot, and enjoyment of the film clip was related strongly to the degree of transportation. Enjoyment was also related to participants' identification with the character of Jack, but less strongly.

EXCITEMENT AND ITS EFFECTS

The anxiety that creates the suspense of a story is a form of excitement. The greater it is, the larger is the relief and satisfaction when it's resolved. You can see this kind of excited anxiety by going to an amusement park that has roller coasters and the like. Watch how people are whirled into the air by elaborate machines. The excitement of being flung about is followed by relief as people get off the ride and talk to their friends. Excitement is on sale in Western society. Television promotes it in its programming and in its advertisements for cars, casinos, sports events, alcohol.

In some action stories and thrillers, excitement and its relief are pretty much the whole content. At the end of stories of this kind, we put down the book or leave the cinema, and apart from a little cardiac consternation, nothing much remains. Such stories are rides on roller coasters.

Many stories have an element of anxious excitement but, in the better ones, the anxiety is the vehicle that takes us into the story world where more significant experiences can occur, experiences that can affect us deeply and personally. Shakespeare's *Hamlet*, is perhaps the most famous literary story in the English speaking world, and it starts by inducing anxiety. Two sentries are on duty in a time of war. In the play's first scene, they each think the other may be the enemy. If the scene is done well, there is an immediate tension. There is a mild relief as the sentries recognize each other. Then the anxiety is ratcheted up again with talk of a ghost. Next there is transformation of the anxiety into questions. What could be the meaning of the ghost's appearance? Now the play really gets going.

In a paper on how we become involved in drama, Dolf Zillmann has explained how this process works. He says that if, in a story, a character whom we like is in danger, we feel anxious. If the character is victimized, we feel affronted on the character's behalf. The process is one of identification and empathy. As Tom Trabasso and Jennifer Chung showed in the experiment that I described in chapter 1, the viewer (or reader) becomes empathetically distressed, and this involves the nervous system becoming excited.[10]

The principle here is that, in the simplest kinds of stories (for instance thrillers), the anxiety, or arousal, or excitement, or interest on behalf of the protagonist will be transformed into relief, a pleasurable emotion. The greater the preceding anxiety, the more eager the page turning and the greater the pleasure of relief. Writers of thrillers know this principle, so they like to crank up their readers' or audience-members' anxiety to as high a level as possible. That is why, in thrillers, we so often encounter psychopathic killers who are about to rape, mutilate, and murder the protagonist's innocent children, and it is why we see so many films in which seconds tick by—with digital clocks counting down—toward the moment when a gigantic thermonuclear explosion will destroy the world.

For "One Another," I hope you will forgive me for not having gone to quite these lengths. There is anxiety, and there is violence in the blow to the back with the butt of a rifle, but the world continues and Alex does not need hospitalization. The anxiety is moderate. Then, as we read part II of the story, there is a moderate relief.

Zillmann pointed out something else about stories. Because excitement decays only gradually, even when the condition that aroused it has ended in one part of a story, some of its effects continue into a new situation in the next part of the story. In part II of "One Another," the new situation is that Alex is back on the train, which crosses the border from Russia into Finland. Alex feels relief. We, too, feel relief on his behalf, and at the same time some of the excited arousal can persist.

For part II of "One Another," I have used this idea, along with one of the most ingenious pieces of social-psychological research I know, which shows something more about effects of continuing excitement. As well as excitement and curiosity continuing in you, the reader (as I hope), I have imagined an excitement for Alex. Inside the world of the story, the arousal of his nervous system continues, from him being taken off the train through to his return, but as it does so, there is a transfer from its original source (being threatened), to something else (attraction to the young woman in his train compartment).

Here's the informative experiment, which was done by Donald Dutton and Arthur Aron. Not far from Vancouver, Canada, where Dutton and Aron worked, is a place called Capilano, where a suspension bridge has been slung high across a gorge, at the bottom of which are the rocks and rapids of the Capilano River. This bridge is 450 feet long. It's very narrow. You cross it by walking on wooden planks suspended from steel cables, onto which you hold anxiously with both hands. It's possible, if you are careful, to let someone pass you in the other direction. But you and the other person hold on tightly to the cables, as this maneuver tends to make the bridge lurch. I have been to Capilano and crossed this bridge. I can confirm that whole thing rocks and sways in an alarming way. Although one knows that really it's safe— this is Canada so that they wouldn't allow anyone on a bridge that was unsafe—nevertheless the swaying and the sight of the rapids and river 200 feet below makes one fear that, with a lurch too many, one will plunge to one's death onto the rocks below. It's what young people call "scary." Upstream, in the same park, is another bridge, down in the valley: a fixed cedar bridge, that is firm, solid, wide, and only 10 feet above the river.

Dutton and Aron had research assistants whose job it was to interview men who walked across either of these two bridges. The men had to be between 18 and 35 and not accompanied by a female. The research assistants were a young and attractive female and a young, no doubt equally attractive, male. The research assistants were not aware of the purpose of the experiment. As each male bridge-crosser reached land on the far side of the bridge, the job of the research assistant was to step forward and ask him to take part in a study she or he was conducting for a psychology class on the subject of scenic attractions. The men were asked to fill out a short questionnaire and respond to a picture of a young woman covering her face with one hand and reaching out with the other. After completing the questions, the research assistant was to thank the man, tear off a corner from a piece of paper, write her or his name and phone number on it, and ask him to phone if he wanted to talk further.

The men who had been met by the female research assistant after they had crossed the high bridge produced more sexual imagery in response to the ambiguous picture than did those who were met by the male research assistant.[11] High marks for sexual imagery were given for any mention of sexual intercourse, and for use of the word *kiss* or *lover*. Sexual imagery in response to the ambiguous picture was far less in those who crossed the low bridge.

Not everyone who was approached agreed to be interviewed, but data were collected from 20 men who agreed after crossing the high scary suspension bridge, and from 20 who crossed the low sturdy bridge. Of the 18 men who had crossed the high bridge and accepted the scrap of paper on which the female research assistant had written her phone number, nine made a phone call to her. This compared with 2 of 16 men who accepted the phone number from the same female research assistant after they had crossed the low bridge.[12] The men's anxious excitement of crossing the high bridge had—with the female interviewer but not the male interviewer—turned into sexual excitement and attraction.

In "One Another," I have suggested that Alex's anxiety at being taken off the train and threatened transforms to a sense of relief as he returns to his compartment, to a sense of friendliness of the other occupants of the compartment, and to sexual attraction to the woman who sits six feet to his left, who by now has taken off her raincoat. She smiles at him, and sits in a posture that gives off a signal of sexual invitation.

I have drawn on another piece of psychological research here: the idea of the sign-stimulus.[13] It has been found that we humans are genetically predisposed to respond to certain patterns in a particular way. If in a lecture, I project onto the screen a picture of a baby with big eyes, I can often hear from the audience the sound "aaah." It's a programmed parental response, more readily made by women than men. If I were to show a picture of a naked woman, another kind of response would tend to be elicited. Pictures of these kinds are called sign-stimuli.

In part II of "One Another," the posture of the young woman as she sits reading her book—her poise, her elongated neck, her silhouetted breast—are sign-stimuli. In Alex, they combine with the excitation, still carrying forward, from his encounter with the border guards. Alex's interest is expressed in his thinking about the woman, imagining her life in Stockholm, imagining that she has recently broken up with an inadequate boyfriend.

Although we sometimes read stories and go to the movies to pass the time, there is also an implicit contract between the writer and reader. If I am a good writer, you will know that everything I write is there because it's integral to the story. So, when in the story you read that Alex starts to think about who the woman might be, as she sits six feet away from him, about what her job may be, about where she lives, and about what her love life may be, you know that these matters are critical parts of the story. They pose certain questions, which you may rely on being taken up as you read on. These questions, too, are part of the suspense.

ONE ANOTHER

PART III

The clacking of wheels slowed, then stopped. They were in Helsinki. The historian rose to lift down her suitcase from the rack. Alex got up immediately to help her with it.

"Thank you," she said. "You're very kind."

The case was large. He pulled it from the rack and set it down for her. It was surprisingly light, with almost nothing in it. He smiled at her, and went to collect his rucksack and anorak.

"Excuse me," he said to the silent Finns.

They smiled at him again.

"Good evening," said the husband. "I wish you a pleasurable stay in Helsinki."

On the platform, Alex said to the young woman: "May I take your case?"

She seemed grateful and they walked toward the main part of the station.

"Are you taking a taxi?" he said.

"I'm at a hotel on the other side of the station square, Hotel Seurahuone."

"Really? I'm staying there too."

They walked across the tram tracks toward the hotel. He stood at a respectful distance behind her as she approached the reception desk. It took just a few moments, and then she waited as he, too, checked in. Politeness: wanting to thank him for carrying her suitcase before saying good night.

He said: "May I buy you a glass of wine, at the bar? In fifteen minutes' time?"

"I'd like that very much."

In his room, Alex locked the door and opened his rucksack. There was the large envelope. He took out the two-inch-thick manuscript, and flicked through it. Exciting. He returned it to its envelope, which he placed upright into the rucksack so that the manuscript would be close to him. It would be a bit of a nuisance, but he'd keep his rucksack with him after he checked out and before the ferry to Stockholm the next day.

Alex carefully repacked his clothes, and put the rucksack in the wardrobe. In the bathroom, he pulled up his shirt to inspect the angry bruise on his back. With a washcloth he bathed it tenderly, and wiped off the smeared blood. He inspected his face in the mirror. Still the same. He looked at his watch. Seven minutes before he'd go down to the bar.

When Alex and the woman met in the bar, she still had on the white blouse she'd worn on the train, still the same skirt, but she'd removed her stockings and changed her shoes to a pair with two-inch heels that made her now almost as tall as him.

"What would you like?"

"You offered a glass of wine, but I don't drink alcohol. May I have a glass of that fruit juice the Finns are so good at."

"Whatever the lady would like by way of fruit juice," said Alex to the barman. "I'll have the same."

They went to sit at a table, by a window that looked out onto the square.

"We've not introduced ourselves. I'm Alex Eklund. I'm half Swedish and half English. I live in London, work in publishing."

"Toril Ericsson. You can tell from my name, I'm completely Swedish," she said. "I live in Stockholm."

"You were doing something exciting in Leningrad?"

"I compose instructions for computers," she said.

"You're a computer programmer."

"Exactly. I have skills that are valuable. They like to hire me there."

Alex studied her face. Her skin was completely clear, not a blemish. She wore no makeup, no earrings. Her nose fascinated him. How could it be so attractive although half pushed to one side?

"You're wondering why I don't get my nose fixed?" she said.

"I find it very attractive."

"You're making fun of me."

"I don't think you should get it fixed. Not at all. I mean it."

"You make a virtue of necessity."

Now, he thought, she's making fun of me. He didn't mind. Her mixture of confidence and warmth enthralled him.

"You're going to Stockholm on the ferry?" he said.

"Tomorrow evening."

"Me too."

"Is that a coincidence, d'you think, going by the ferry?"

"Unless you believe in certain things."

"Certain things?"

"Synchronicity," he said.

"Is that what it's called?"

Suddenly it seemed very funny, and they both laughed.

"You're a publisher who lives in London, with a wife and a three-year-old son," she said.

"No marks for the first part because I already told you, and no marks for the second part. No wife, no children."

Alex started to talk about how he'd been a stockbroker, and how he'd found it empty. Because he'd always loved books, he'd thought of publishing, and been helped by a friend who'd taught him the ropes. At a certain moment, Alex sensed a current between them, distinct, palpable. He looked at her, intently, to see if she had felt it too. He sensed that she had. She smiled, an expression of extraordinary warmth and then, as if embarrassed, she cast her eyes down.

"Here we are in a bar, in front of a window that looks onto a public square," he said. "I wonder if we might adjourn to somewhere more private."

"I was thinking the same."

Alex had barely touched his fruit juice, and Toril seemed not to have started hers. They got up from the table, crossed the lobby, and mounted the curved staircase to the second floor. Along the corridor a little, Alex opened the door to his room, switched on the light, and held the door open for her.

She walked several steps into the room and turned toward him. He moved to her and stopped when he was close. She glanced into his eyes, then looked carefully at the buttons of his shirt. His top button was undone. He wasn't wearing a tie. Carefully she undid the second button. She undid each one, and pulled up the part of the shirt that was tucked in his trousers. She opened it so that his chest was bare. Then she looked down at her white blouse. The top buttons were already undone, She started to undo lower buttons, one by one, down to the last. She opened her blouse, moved toward him. In the train she must have been wearing a bra. Not now. Against his chest, he felt the slightly erect nipple of her right breast, the one he had admired. She moved it a little, not pushing into him but hovering, stroking him gently. It was the most erotic thing he'd ever experienced. It moved him more than he was prepared for. By then her mouth was on his. They took two steps toward the bed.

Almost before knowing it, clothes were discarded, and they were both underneath a soft duvet, in each other's arms. They fitted perfectly together. He felt her skin against his, from the lips which touched, to the breasts that now pressed gently against his chest, and to those lower parts that seemed alive, and down further to a foot that she had twined round his ankle. With his left arm he was able to stroke her back, up to the nape of her neck. With her right arm she stroked his back and neck, stroked with lingering gentleness.

"Sorry, I must put a thing on," he said.

Slowly, slowly, they moved together, and she welcomed him. It was as if they barely had to move at all and the feelings became infinite. She pressed toward him, enabling him to think that what she wanted most in the world was him, there. What he wanted was her, there, in just this way. A feeling of generosity welled through him, a knowledge that he would do anything for her, and in a little while she began to move in a distinctive way, with her arm now behind his waist, and pulling him toward her until, with a delicate sigh, she came. So profound was the feeling of their closeness that he felt himself coming, too. He could not have prevented it. It enveloped him. It was not something happening to him. It was not even in him. It was between them, joining them a way that he knew it was what the world had been made for.

They lay still for some time, holding hands. Then he pulled her toward him, so that she laid her head on his neck, and so that he could have his arm around her and gently stroke her hair.

"We are good together," she said.

"More than good."

"You're very containing," she said. "Most men are more aggressive."

"Most men?" he said.

She held up an index finger to his lips, then reached again for his hand and squeezed it, and continued to hold it, childlike, very close.

For ten minutes, they lay quietly.

"You were looking at me in the train," she said.

"You were looking at me."

"I'm glad we looked."

"Me too."

"The world we live in is very difficult," she said.

"Was this so difficult?"

She was silent again, for a long time. She seemed about to say something important.

"You don't realize how fortunate you are to live in England."

"As compared with Sweden?"

There was another pause, a long pause.

"Come here. I want to nuzzle your neck," she said.

As the skin of their bodies touched, he felt himself stir once more. Without saying anything, as if it were the most ordinary of actions, she had found another prophylactic from the bedside table, reached down, rolled it onto him, and put him inside her, where it was warm, a perfect place. They took their time until he felt her moving again. He held her, as she grasped strongly onto him.

They lay quiet for while. "I'm going to come over there now," she said.

She came to hover over him.

Chapter 3

Falling in Love

To fall in love is to extend one's self to enclose another person. Love stories are fascinating because of the question of how we might know whom we might join in this all-engaging way. Fantasy is a strong component both of falling in love and the stories to which this state gives rise.

Worldwide, as Patrick Hogan has shown, the commonest kind of story is about love. "One Another" started off as a suspense story, but in part III it seems suddenly to turn into a love story. Alex's interest is caught by a woman with whom he sat for a few hours in a train. He expresses the interest by lifting down her suitcase from the luggage rack, carrying it for her, inviting her for a drink in a hotel bar, where they talk for a bit, and he feels that very special kind of current between them that we call falling in love. The word *falling* has a special meaning: a quality not of something one does but of something that happens.

Rasa theorists argued that literary works should be based on one *rasa* at a time, and this idea corresponds to the idea of genres in the West: love stories, comedies, tragedies, and so forth. These theorists also described how, although there should be a principal focus on one *rasa*, the plot should also pass through other *rasas*, as well as transitional phases such as apprehension and bewilderment. Because this book is about the emotions of fiction, I wanted to cover a representative number of emotions.

I knew, therefore, as I was writing "One Another," that I'd need the story to move through several *rasas*. The story starts with the *rasa* of the heroic in part I—Alex sets out on his plan to smuggle a document—and moves to the amorous in part II, as Alex notices the young woman wearing a white blouse, and this theme continues into part III, in which he and the woman make love.

I chose Leo Tolstoy's novel *Anna Karenina* for Alex to read on the train because, although I worried that it might be bulky for the pocket of an anorak, I wanted to foreshadow the move to the amorous. In Tolstoy's novel this occurs with Anna's rather incomplete commitment to her husband, Karenin, and hence her susceptibility to Vronsky's advances.[1] This offers a parallel to Alex's inner doubts in his relationship with Sonya, which make him susceptible to the events that occur in part III of this story.

SUGGESTIVENESS AND THE EROTIC

For the Indian idea of *rasas*, an important theorist was Abhinavagupta, who wrote 1,000 years ago in a royal court in the area that is now Kashmir. He gives the following example of a verse from a play, of how the *rasa* of the amorous can work. In the play, a young woman's husband is away. A traveler arrives at her house, and she invites him to stay. Here's what the young woman says to the traveler.

> Mother-in-law sleeps here, I there:
> Look, traveler, while it is light.
> For at night when you cannot see
> You must not fall into my bed.[2]

The verse works by *dhvani*—suggestion—we might even say suggestiveness. An intuition of love has passed between the young woman and the traveler. This little verse seems rather literal, without metaphors. Abhinavagupta discusses how, in it, the young woman speaks openly in the presence of her mother-in-law and, by means of a prohibition, she makes the traveler an invitation. If he does not understand it, he misses an opportunity. If we readers or audience members do not understand it, we can have it explained to us, and Abhinavagupta gives us several pages of such explanation. Within the *rasa* of the erotic we might notice that, in what the young woman says, there are *double entendres*: "sleep" and "bed." There is a contrast between "light" when the young woman is talking, in which relationships are public, polite, and observable, and the "night" to come, a setting for the private in which, moreover, one may not be able to see properly not only because of the darkness but because of being blinded by love. If you enter the *rasa* of the amorous, then, as you watch and listen to the scene in which this verse occurs, you can intuit some of the excitement and anticipation between the young woman and the traveler, perhaps based on your own experiences of sexual attraction, perhaps from having read or seen other literary love scenes.

In modern theater, *rasas* have been adapted for the training of actors with the idea of Rasaboxes,[3] a set of boxes drawn on the studio floor rather like squares for hopscotch. Each box represents one *rasa*. Actors are invited draw on all the knowledge they have of the emotion, including memories from their lives. When they are in training, actors step into one of the boxes, and imagine the *rasa* it represents taking over not just their mind but their body. In the Rasabox of the furious, the actor does not just prepare to behave in a furious fashion, he or she might become flushed, eyes wide and staring, fists clenched, heart pounding.

At a conference in New York, a drama trainer who trained actors using this technique said that as she stepped into the Rasabox of the amorous, she would feel her nipples becoming erect.

The amorous or erotic is a distinctive genre of fiction. One of its best writers, in my view, was Anaïs Nïn who, for a while, earned her living by writing erotic stories. The purpose of such stories is to produce sexual arousal in the reader, which, perhaps like the excitement of suspense, is one of those pleasurable emotional states that we enter as a distraction from other matters or when, for whatever reason, there's no possibility of our own erotic encounter with a lover.

In writing this section, I am all too aware that the erotic episode I have written in "One Another" is from Alex's male point of view. So here, to compare, is a passage from a female perspective by another psychologist who writes fiction, Elaine Hatfield, from her novel *Rosie* (written in collaboration with her husband, Richard Rapson).

Three kisses and Rosie was drunk with love, cheeks flushed, lips coral and bruised. Now Rosie was lost to reason. Now she would be willing to give Mike absolutely anything he wanted. He could kiss, caress, touch, and taste.

Rosie gave a little shiver of delight and Mike watched a kaleidoscope of emotion waft over her face, as uncensored as a breeze. Rosie was a nightblooming Cereus, a little nest of yearning, her hips pushing up toward him, opening up to him.

Rosie moaned, ecstasy masquerading as misery. Mike and Rosie swayed together, dancing in an echoing tintenabulum of sound.

A breathy rustle of delight.

A muffled catch in the throat.

A sob of pleasure.

An ancient, archaic cry; a mournful Alexandrine lament of love, and loss.

Then it was over. (p. 139).

Hatfield and Rapson are more exotic in their metaphors and verbal associations than I have been in the scene in "One Another," but I don't think the atmosphere in *Rosie* is much different from that of Alex's hotel room in Hotel Seurohuone. I also don't believe that homosexual episodes would be so very different, in fact I wrote such episodes in my first novel, *The Case of Emily V.*

Pornography is based on display of sexual sign-stimuli (as explained in chapter 2) in language or pictures without any thought that what is displayed are aspects of another person. Pornography also derives from a propensity we—especially the males of our species—share with bonobos, our closest relations among the apes, to enjoy witnessing sexual signs and sexual activity. I wish I could say more on the subject, but I'm sorry that, apart from these derivations, I can't think of anything.

The amorous or erotic, I think, is different. There is sex, and with the proper amount of *dhvani* (the suggestive) it can be arousing. It takes place between a character such as a protagonist and someone with whom that character joins in something that involves both, together. Alex experiences it as a current of love, and feels generosity toward Toril. One has to be careful with whom one makes love. In her theory of why sex really can be a making of love, Elaine Hatfield (author of the love-scene I have just quoted) suggested another version of the transfer of excitement idea. One tends to attribute the excitement and delight of sex to that other person.[4] It's a powerful effect. If it wouldn't be a good idea to fall in love with someone, you should think twice, or more than twice, about having sex with that person.

A SCRIPT FOR FALLING IN LOVE

In chapter 2, I discussed the idea that sometimes emotions are not just incidents. They can be sequences of actions and events, based on scripts. The idea of the heroic—leaving on a journey, facing dangers, returning home with valuable knowledge—is an example. The script tells us what to expect. It instills protagonists and audiences with courage to face dangers, and with a sense of perseverance.

Falling in love is also based on a script. As Nico Frijda has described,[5] it, too, has a sequence. It, too, is widely known by people in our culture.

Here is the falling-in-love script as it appears in William Shakespeare's *Romeo and Juliet*. Two people are young and open to a sexual encounter. They are strangers to each other. Romeo sees Juliet across a room, and is attracted. No words are exchanged. There is then an interval during which he thinks about her. The two then meet face to face, and they talk in a way that confirms each one's interest in the other. Already, they are toppling into that state of falling in love, a state that will be experienced as all absorbing, all sufficient, and enough to annul all former commitments.

If a writer depicts this sequence or even a part of it, it's enough to carry our understanding of the whole script. In "One Another" for instance, we can as readers connect the opening stages for Alex, of being open to a sexual encounter, with our knowledge that he doesn't find everything in his relationship with Sonya to be as he wants it. As readers, we can understand that running the love script can be sufficient for Alex to overlook his commitment to Sonya and to fall in love with Toril.

The idea of a script helps us to see, I think, why the Indian idea of *rasas* such as the amorous can be powerful not just in literature, but in life. As Alex steps his way through the script of falling in love, he is caught up in a potent fantasy about a person about whom—after all—he knows almost nothing. In literature, too, the idea helps us to see why a *rasa* can be suggestive. Once embarked on a *rasa* of the amorous, it's the implications of love that come to mind. The word *fall*,[6] for instance, is suggestive of the idea of the involuntary aspects of falling in love.

Scripts of the amorous enable us to visit worlds of love, and to take rides on the vehicles that transport us into those worlds. The idea of script works perfectly with the idea of story, which is also a sequence of actions and outcomes. One of the functions of stories is to enable enjoyable resonances with certain familiar scripts. In psychological understandings of love, the idea has been taken a step further by Robert Sternberg in his book *Love Is a Story*, in which he argues that, to understand anyone's love relationship, one has to understand what kind of story it has at its center. Perhaps the story is of two friends who join together to strive against difficulties; perhaps it's of a master and slave; perhaps it's of a state of competition and skirmishing; perhaps it's of each person's addiction to the other.

FANTASY IN STORIES

One kind of love story is the most successful genre of all. It's the romance story, and the acknowledged leader in this field is the publisher Harlequin.[7] At the beginning of September 2010, I visited their web site I found this to be their featured book at the time, in the Harlequin Romance series: *Australia's Most Eligible Bachelor*, by Margaret Way. Here is the puff. "Corin Rylance is super-handsome, super-rich and sets women's hearts aflutter! Miranda Thornton is no exception. She secretly loves Corin, but, raised as a farmer's daughter, she's hardly a match for Australia's most eligible bachelor! Corin's sister takes Miranda under her wing and she gets to sample their glittering lifestyle—sipping champagne and dining in the finest restaurants. But it's the tingles and electricity that sizzle when Corin is near that really make this ordinary girl feel like a million dollars..."

Some critics argue that such romance stories are entirely formulaic, that they discourage thought, and appeal to childish fantasies. Fantasies are not, however, to be sneered at, and romances are instructive for understanding the emotional appeal of stories. The best study of romances and their fantasy qualities that I know is by Janice Radway. She made contact with a woman who worked in a chain bookstore in a midwestern American town, whom she calls Dot, who enjoyed romances, thought about them, was consulted by her customers, and wrote a newsletter to review the stories. Radway distributed a questionnaire to 50 romance readers who were Dot's customers, and received back 42 replies. She was also able to interview 16 of them in person. Radway starts her book with a quotation from a letter sent by a romance reader to Harlequin Enterprises that was representative of how her interviewees felt.

I am twenty-five, a wife and mother. Sometimes, like so many other people, I get low in spirits. Maybe from reading the paper, from an encounter with someone hateful, whatever. I can pick up one of her [Essie Summers's] books and see goodness staring out at me. The heroine makes me feel it's a lovely world, people are good, one can face anything and we are lucky to be alive. What a wonderful feeling ... and if it wasn't for Harlequin, I'd never know this uplift ... Your books stand for decency and beliefs. That's rare these days.

Dot's customers agreed that to read romances is to indulge in a fantasy. Only a proportion of them thought the people they read about were like people they met in everyday life. The most striking conclusion in Radway's book is that in reading romances during their busy lives as wives and mothers, women were asserting their claim to have something of their own, in which mentally they could absent themselves from their perpetual responsibilities. For these women, the center of a romance was a relationship in which, after misunderstanding, or even after the hero had behaved badly (in a male sort of way), the heroine comes to be loved by him, and cared for by him, for herself. When the sexual act occurs, the heroine can give herself up to it in complete trust. In other words, in a romance of this kind, the female protagonist comes to be cared for in the kind of way in which she cares for members of her family, and in a way that enables her to keep doing that.

Since Radway's book, much research has been done on the topic of romances and their appeal. Among recent writers are Laura Vivanco and Kyra Kramer who have proposed that a recurring theme in romances is transformation. They see this as continuing to occur, from early romances such as Jane Austen's *Pride and Prejudice* onward. Although Austen writes of Mr. Darcy's "utmost force of passion," he is not complete as a person. He is rich and high born, but his pride prevents him from being a fully formed man. The story is about how Elizabeth Bennet, with her intelligence and determination, accomplishes a transformation of Darcy, so that he becomes able to admit his shortcomings, to become more aware of others, and to become capable of intimacy. At the same time, Elizabeth's own prejudices are confronted. However, it's only when Darcy's pride is transformed that Elizabeth will marry him. Vivanco and Kramer use the metaphor of alchemy for this theme. Instead of the older male alchemist who, by means of the philosopher's stone, sought to transform base metal into gold, the newer female alchemist, by means of her sexual power, becomes able to transform the imperfect male into gold.

For the understanding of emotions in fiction, I think we can say that each popular genre—heroic adventure, romance, drama, mystery—seems to be based on a core fantasy.

In a heroic adventure, the core fantasy was discerned by Sigmund Freud, in one of his earliest articles on literature: entitled "Creative writers and daydreaming." He starts his article like this.

> We laymen have always been intensely curious to know...
> from what sources that strange being, the creative writer,
> draws his material, and how he manages to make such an
> impression on us with it and to arouse in us emotions of
> which, perhaps, we had not even thought ourselves capable
> (p. 131).

The answer, says Freud, is that the stories that arouse such emotions are expressions of wishes. That is to say, they are like dreams, the meanings of which—according to Freud—are also expressions of wishes. Just as dreams have to be disguised because they would affront us with their sexual self-centeredness or their violence if their meanings were explicit, so stories involve a certain amount of disguise, for instance by displacement from oneself to literary characters. Freud points out that if, at the end of a chapter in a story, one reads that the hero is "unconscious and bleeding from severe wounds, [one is] sure to find him at the beginning of the next being carefully nursed and on the way to recovery" (p. 137). Although, in such stories, dangers are depicted, one can read about them with a sense of perfect security, because, in the hidden layers of our minds, the plots indulge us in what we wish for: to triumph over those who oppose us and to be tenderly cared for. If, in adulthood, we were to put this to ourselves or others in raw form, we would laugh—because it is so childish. But, says Freud, the skill of the writer is such that, transmuted into story form, we can indulge such fantasies acceptably.

The heroic story is predominantly male, and it's read or watched mostly by men. One may say that a lot of men work hard and continuously, although for the most part their job—insurance salesman, truck driver, office worker—may not seem very adventurous. Reading about the heroic or watching a hero at the movies can give people the mental possibility of being heroic.

The romance is predominantly female, and it's read or watched mostly by women. For women who are mothers, and who look after their family, their day-to-day experience is caring for others, despite the fact that their activities and love may not always be recognized and despite long stretches of drudgery. What Janice Radway found is that women in her study knew that to read romances was to enter a fantasy world in which they (the readers) could be loved by a sexual partner in the way that the readers wanted to be loved—for themselves.

There seems, however, to be a curious feature: perhaps both these genres are more sexually ambiguous than one might think. In the heroic story, after they have encountered danger, tough guys are often attended by women. One might think they simply have sex, but the more discerning reader will know that what's really going on is that the men are cared for. In the romance, before she is loved, the woman protagonist needs to be heroic, to strive and face dangers of standing up for herself against an insensitive, sometimes bullying, man. Only by her efforts is the man transformed into someone capable of caring for her.

One might propose, as a hypothesis, that for each genre, there is different core fantasy and that, perhaps as the Indian *rasa* theorists proposed, each is based on a particular kind of emotional script: heroic courage, love, and so forth.

In the genre of drama or action story, the *rasa* is anger, or, as the Sanskrit theorists say, the furious. The core fantasy is one of conflict at the end of which the protagonist will triumph. Frequently, the story starts with the protagonist being victimized. The reader or audience member becomes angry and vengeful and, within the anger script, good triumphs, in the end, over wickedness and cruelty. This kind of story can, of course, be easily melded with a story of the heroic.

A story based on detection (sometimes called a mystery story) seems also to depend on its own underlying fantasy. This genre has its own set of fans, and recent publishing successes by writers like Dan Brown and Stieg Larsson testify to the interest it can elicit. At first sight, detective stories, or detective thrillers, seem not to be as directly based on an emotion or *rasa* as stories of heroism and romance. What they are about, after all, is a train of clues and a process of detection. Even so, there is an underlying fantasy, which I first heard explained 25 years ago at an event in the Edinburgh Festival at which detective-story writer,

P.D. James, spoke. What happens in this kind of story, she said, is that damage has been caused to the fabric of society, so that things no longer work as they should. Prototypically, of course, there's been a murder. Then a mysterious figure—a Sherlock Holmes or a Hercule Poirot[8]—with almost godlike qualities of ratiocination appears and is able, by mere brain power, to discern what happened and by doing so to mend the damage to society in such a way that ordinary life can resume. In other words, the mystery is a species of drama, based on the *rasa* of the furious— anger. The detective does not express anger as such. He or she maintains an other-worldly serenity, and transmutes societal anger to unfold for us the outrage to human decency that has occurred. By bringing the criminal to justice, he or she enacts vengeance on our behalf. This genre, too, seems to tickle what Dolf Zillmann has pointed out: our propensity to be moral monitors. It's a role that seems never to pall.

Therefore, it is not only the heroic and the amorous that are based on underlying scripts, which in turn are each based on an underlying fantasy and emotion. One could work through the *rasas* in the table that I gave in chapter 1 and think about the genre to which each gives rise. One could think, too, for each *rasa*, what its underlying fantasy might be.

PART IV

What's the time? Alex reached toward Toril, to touch her arm, to feel her there among the dark folds of the duvet. Nothing. Suddenly he was awake. He reached to turn on the light, and looked around the room. Not there. He got out of bed, naked. Not in the bathroom. Hurriedly he put on his yesterday clothes.

Where was she? Gone back to her room? Past seven o'clock. She'd gone down to breakfast. She'd be sitting there, near the window. She would raise her eyes from her coffee as he entered the room, and she would smile.

In the breakfast room, she wasn't there. He walked round the room twice, to make sure. People stared at him. He ran up the curving staircase to his room again. Still she wasn't there. He looked round the room. He looked on the desk. She'd not left a note. He didn't even know her room number. He went downstairs again, went to the reception desk. Would they tell him her room number?

The receptionist was the man who'd checked them in.

"The woman I arrived with last night," he said. "She was a friend."

He hesitated, thought he might stammer.

"We'd arranged to see each other this morning. Can you tell me her room number."

He blushed. The receptionist noticed, which intensified the hot red feeling about his neck.

"I'm sorry sir. Your friend left this morning. About five-thirty."

"Thank you."

He walked away from the desk, then returned.

"Did she call a taxi?"

"There are taxis across the road, at the station. I asked her if she would like help with her luggage. She said she would manage by herself."

"Did she leave a message?"

"No message, Sir."

Alex stumbled upstairs, back into his room, lay on his bed. A wave swept over him. Desolation. At last he had met that certain person. Now she'd vanished. Was she all right? Why didn't she leave a note? At half-past ten, he was due to meet a Finnish publisher, then a publisher in Stockholm tomorrow. Could anything be so irrelevant?

He washed and shaved and brushed his teeth. He went to the wardrobe, took out his rucksack, found clean underpants, a clean shirt.

Where was the manuscript? He emptied everything onto the bed. The manuscript was gone.

In a frenzy, he ran down to the reception desk.

"Sorry," he said. "My friend and I were in the bar for fifteen minutes last night. Could anyone have gone into my room at that time? Anyone at all?"

"I don't think so sir. You had the key with you. You didn't give it to me when you came down."

"Sorry...I had to ask."

"Something is lost?"

"Something valuable."

"Would you like me to phone the police?"

"No, not yet. Thank you."

Back in his room, he lay on the bed.

There was someone who'd been in his room last night. Toril. She had taken the manuscript. A wave of anger invaded him. The military presence at the border, the blow in the back with the rifle butt. It was still painful. It was a set-up. She was with the KGB. "We know everything"—that's what they said—"We want to save you from yourself."

But between Toril and him? With that closeness? That was worth something...it was worth everything. Why didn't she leave a note? A scrap of paper, a few words: "They have me." To let him know. But there was no note.

Now he was really angry.

He walked to the harbor, to the ferry terminal, to ask whether a Toril Ericsson was booked for Stockholm that evening. No. The next evening? No. She'd lied to him about taking the ferry to Stockholm. He walked back to the hotel.

He'd been played. The whole thing was a set-up. She wasn't from Stockholm. She was hired by the KGB to work as a prostitute. The headscarf when he'd got into the train, then the long neck, the white blouse carefully chosen to show off the profile of that far-too-desirable breast. And the suitcase. It had almost nothing in it. That was a tip-off. Why didn't he think? And the drink at the bar. He'd thought that he'd made the moves. That's how they do it, these people. They make you think it's you making the decisions. And the love making. Trained for that kind of thing.

After they'd made love for the first time, he'd had a thought about Sonya, wondered why sex with her wasn't like this. He'd banished the thought from his mind. Now he knew why it had been perfect. It was a piece of theater: perfectly staged, perfectly directed, perfectly acted.

Alex lay on his bed, inspected a crack in the ceiling that he hadn't noticed. His face set into hard stone. He clenched his jaw. If there was one thing he'd never been able to stand, it was being taken for a ride, played for a sucker. She'd be in a car now, with her handler, already across the border. Had the handler been booked into the hotel, too? Or, if the whole thing wasn't too important to them, she'd be alone, returning on the train they'd come on, which would have left for Leningrad early this morning. He looked at his watch. Should he hire a taxi? Try to overtake the train. It didn't go very fast. He jumped from the bed, ran downstairs, out of the hotel, across tram tracks to the station, and found the timetable for the trains. It was nearly half-past eight. The train would be almost at the border. No chance of catching it.

Perhaps it wasn't her who'd taken the manuscript. Perhaps it was the hotel receptionist. They must have several keys for each room. He could be an agent of the Soviets. The man had sneaked upstairs when he and Toril were in the bar. Perhaps her minder who'd booked into the hotel earlier had picked the lock of his room. Could that have been it? Possible, but she was in on the scheme. Otherwise he wouldn't have gone to the bar. If he'd stayed in his room and gone to bed, he'd still have the manuscript. Of course it was her. It all made sense—from the Finland Station to her slipping out of the hotel in the early morning.

How could he catch up with her? He would grasp her upper arms roughly, bruising them, shake her. He'd shout: "How could you? After what was between us? How could you?" It was hopeless. The Soviet Union was vast, its apparatus impenetrable.

And the manuscript? They must have known about it all along. How stupid he'd been to think he might be followed to the station. But then, from the train compartment onwards, all the information had been right there in front of him. He'd thought of it in one configuration, when really it was in another. Would one really meet someone who just might be the love of one's life by chance? And would there really be a coincidence of such a rare event with his plan to smuggle a unique document out of Russia? And would one know the love of one's life when a horrible headscarf and a miserable macintosh were removed to reveal blond hair, a long neck, and a beautiful breast? Weren't such sexual fantasies rather common, rather easy to enact? Now, it was clear; the whole pattern, simple but clear.

And David! He'd be furious.

Back in his hotel room: despair. She had loved him. It was brief, yes, but for both of them it was that one moment in life for which we all long. She didn't dare say anything. It would be too dangerous for her to leave a note. He thought again of Sonya and her ailing mother. Toril must have a mother, perhaps a child. Unless she did exactly what they demanded, her mother and her child would disappear and she'd never see them again.

These thoughts were worse. In anger there's a certain self-righteousness. But the desolation of loss. What could assuage it?

Had she put something in his drink? No that wasn't it: he'd barely touched it. She must have left when he fell asleep, after they'd made love the second time. He'd read something about how the male orgasm produces the profoundest sleep. That's why she wanted to do it again. She must have got out of bed without making a sound, pulled on her skirt and blouse, found the manuscript in his rucksack, gone to her room, planned to leave the hotel at dawn.

He shut his eyes and imagined her, opening the door noiselessly so that the latch did not click, her shoes in one hand, manuscript under her arm, looking to make sure he didn't stir.

He lay on his bed, found himself in tears, unbearable tears. That kind of closeness almost never happens.

Why had he not thought? If he'd stayed awake, he could have stopped her sneaking off with the manuscript. If he'd thought about it properly, realized in the train that she was putting on a show, realized there was something wrong with her suitcase being too light, realized when she said he was lucky to be living in England, she wasn't comparing it to Sweden but to the USSR.

He'd let her remark go. She was putting out a feeler. She was signaling to him that she was acting under duress. Why didn't he realize? Nothing bad could happen to them in Helsinki. They could have gone back to England together. She could have applied for asylum, or whatever you have to do.

Perhaps she didn't fully realize. So vanishingly rare: that chance when people truly match, when each can be what the other yearns for. That state that takes one out of oneself, that is bigger than any of us. It was a chance, and he'd missed it. She'd missed it. They'd both missed it.

He was in tears again, supine on that same bed on which they'd made love, in that same containing room. And, despite the pain of loss, he felt himself suffused once more by the feeling of the night before, the feeling of closeness that comes just once in a life, but never when one expects it, because it can't be willed. Was he fortunate perhaps that it had come to him? Even if so briefly. Or was it to bring him a lesson? Something about himself and Sonya, that the experience—whatever it was—visits a person only for a moment. It emphasizes its own transience, its almost-hallucinatory quality. To accept Sonya, to love her properly, he must accept that this was ephemeral. Accept it deeply, in the core of himself.

Chapter 4

Loss and Sadness

Sadness is the principal emotion of reflection, when a loss has occurred. It's a state in which one can look back to see how one has reached the predicament one is in and to think, too, what the implications might be.

Love is a joining together. Making love is the very emblem of common purpose with another. It's a center of marriage, which, in the West at least, is a defining state of cooperation in a life. In sexual love, the self extends to enclose the other person within the circle of selfhood.

I mentioned in chapter 3 that, in writing "One Another," I knew would need to visit several *rasas*, in order to range across a representative set of the emotions of fiction. In part IV of "One Another" the joining-together of Alex and Toril is broken by Toril. Such a break gives rise, in Alex, to certain emotions: sadness, a sense of betrayal, shame, anger.

Sadness is a state of drawing back, of disengagement from a relationship or project that is lost, a state of reflection.

For the reader of "One Another?" how do we feel when we realize that Toril has not only run off, but has stolen the manuscript? How do we feel when we realize that the state of togetherness that Alex experienced with her is lost, and was, on her part, a ruse?

In part I of the story, the antagonist was represented by border guards with rifles. Now it becomes clear that real antagonist in the story is Toril.

In classic European detective stories, the detective enjoys an immunity from destructive forces, but in the kind of detective fiction pioneered by Dashiell Hammett (for instance in *The Maltese Falcon*) and Raymond Chandler (for instance in *The Big Sleep*) the detective is no longer immune. The forces of the antagonists are such that he (usually he) will be threatened with firearms, beaten up, confined, humiliated. At the same time, he also is not immune from forces of sexuality, so that often, as we read or watch a detective story, we are not sure what to make of an alluring woman to whom the detective is sexually drawn. Such a woman, to whom the protagonist makes love, is generally thought, because of the love making, to be an ally, but she can turn out to be an antagonist. This is what happens in "One Another." Unlike the way in which the antagonism usually occurs in hard-boiled stories, however, the means used by the antagonist in this story do not include guns or blunt instruments. The means Toril uses can wound the soul.

In my view, then, this is where "One Another" becomes (as it were) more serious. A change of key occurs, to sadness, a more reflective emotion than anger. In terms of the *rasas* that I introduced in chapter 1, we enter the state of the pitiable or tragic.

Alex started off on the path of a hero, but he fails, and beneath that failure is another. He fails Sonya, too, by having an affair. His impulsiveness, his sense of himself as attractive, confronts him, not only with the loss of a manuscript, but also with other losses that are more significant: a loss within himself as he realizes he has betrayed Sonya. Without it needing to be said explicitly, we all know that such a betrayal opens the possibility for a loss of Sonya, too. This presents a paradox, I think. How do we as readers feel about Alex the protagonist behaving badly?

Whereas romances, action stories, and mystery stories, lend themselves to popular forms in books and movies, stories of sadness are less popular, perhaps because, as the romance readers interviewed by Janice Radway explained, they don't end with the reader feeling that all is right with the world. Neither do sad stories necessarily end in the way that adventure and action stories do, with the hero succeeding or with a satisfying retribution for the wickedness of others having been exacted.

EMOTIONS DIRECT OUR THINKING

Anger and sadness are both forms of distress. If anger focuses on the outer world and what to do about a humiliation or hurt, sadness focuses on the inner world and on our own responsibility for what happened. Sad stories encourage us to reflect not only on the situation in the story, but on our own life.

Here is a study that Seema Nundy and I did on differences between anger and sadness in reading Russell Banks's short story, "Sarah Cole: A Type of Love Story."[1] The story is told by a male narrator, who says that, at the time of the story's events, he was "extremely handsome." He also says that Sarah was "the homliest woman" he had ever known. He explains that, in the story, he will just call himself "the man," and that he is describing the events 10 years after they happened. The affair starts when Sarah sees the man in a bar and the friends she is with suggest she tries to pick him up. She does so. An affair begins, and it continues for several months. The man ends the affair in a cruel way, with him saying: "Leave me now, you disgusting, ugly bitch."

Nundy and I gave readers a list of emotion words: happiness, sadness, anger, fear, and so forth. We asked them to use a scale of 0 to 10 to rate how intensely they were feeling each one. Then, we asked them to read the story. Then, we gave them the list of emotions for a second time, and asked them again to rate the intensity of each. For each reader, we found which emotion had undergone the largest change from before to after reading. The story is unusual in that it gives rise to different emotions in different readers. In our study, some readers became mainly sad, some became mainly angry, and some became mainly disgusted.

After they finished the story, we asked the readers three interpretive questions about its ambiguous ending. Our first question was:, "From the narrator's point of view, why do you think the story says, 'She's transformed into the most beautiful woman he has ever seen?'" Here's an example of a response.

> He no longer sees Sarah as belonging to him. She breaks away from him probably more strongly than he tries to separate from her. He is also not truly capable of a true respectful love…and maybe feels guilty and envious that she was giving in the relationship he was never honestly in.

We classified readers' responses by the kind of reasoning they did. In this case the reader starts with the conclusion, "He no longer sees Sarah as belonging to him," which is this reader's answer to the question about why she seemed so beautiful. Then, this reader gives a set of reasons for the conclusion: "She breaks away from him…He is not truly capable…maybe feels guilty and envious." In cognitive psychology this kind of reasoning, starting with a conclusion and then giving reasons for it, is called backward chaining.

Here is an example of a response to our second question, which was: "From the narrator's point of view, why do you think the story says, 'It's not as if she had died; it's as if he has killed her?'" Here is part of another reader's response.

> He knew she knew and everyone else [knew] that she was "homely." Perhaps it was perverse or pity that he engaged in a relationship with her. But despite her physical appearance, which she struggled with, she had feelings...So out of guilt he might as well have killed emotionally—cut deep into the soul at any rate.

This reader starts with ideas from the beginning of the story, that both the man and Sarah knew she was "homely" then moves forward, via intermediate ideas, for instance, that Sarah "had feelings," toward the conclusion—the answer to the question about why the story said "it's as if he has killed her"—that "he might as well have killed her emotionally." In cognitive psychology this kind of reasoning is called forward chaining.

We found that people's predominant emotion in reading the story predicted how they reasoned. Those who became sad on reading "Sarah Cole" reasoned predominantly by backward chaining: they started with a conclusion and reasoned backwards to why it had come about. In sadness one starts from a state of loss or disappointment, and then thinks backward reflectively to understand how it came about, and what one might have done to cause it.

By contrast, those who became angry on reading the story reasoned mainly by forward chaining. In anger one thinks forward from the current situation toward the future, for instance about how to achieve retribution, to get even with the person who has been hurtful. It was interesting to us to find that, when people experienced anger in reading, this set them predominantly into this forward-thinking mode, which they displayed in answering our questions.[2]

So the way each reader thought about this story was affected by the emotion he or she experienced, and these emotions were very much the readers' own. The way participants thought about the story was also their own, and was affected by their predominant emotion.

In "One Another," I have tried to balance the possibility that Alex feels mainly sad in his experience with Toril with the possibility that he feels mainly angry. I've written the story to leave open how you, the reader, might feel about its events. How you feel is likely to influence your interpretation of the story.

SOMETHING BIGGER THAN OURSELVES

In day-to-day life, sadness tends to occur with a loss: we become sad and tearful when someone close dies, when a loved one upsets us, or when some aspiration is disappointed. But we can also find ourselves in tears in a work of fiction. I watched Michael Curtiz's film *Casablanca* again recently and found myself in tears at the touching reconciliation between the Humphrey Bogart character (Rick) and the Ingrid Bergman character (IIsa), not, I think, because of the loss, although at the end of the film they do lose each other, but because they do the right thing by parting.

Tears at the movies are often regarded as sentimental: a derogatory term used to dismiss an experience as immature and stupid. It's not been much discussed in research. The best paper I know on the subject of being tearful at the movies is by Ed Tan and Nico Frijda who propose that this kind of experience is important and that it signifies that we are taken out of our usual self-centered perspective. We cry in the closing scenes of *Casablanca*, or of *Hamlet*, or of *Anna Karenina*, not so much because of a loss, but because we feel ourselves in the presence of something larger than ourselves, something that takes us out of our egoistic concerns, something that prompts reflectiveness, something that makes room for insight.

An important example of something larger than ourselves is the theme of attachment. Attachment is the state, first recognized by John Bowlby, of relating as infants to our caregivers. It's a biologically given state in mammals, the psychological equivalent of the physiological processes of being born live and of being suckled with milk. The genetic program of attachment keeps the mother or other caregiver close to the infant, to protect and nurture it. For infants, the genetic program prompts them to make a terrible fuss when the caregiver isn't available, and later, when the infant can move about, to keep close to the caregiver. For most of us, the attachment relationship was, at one time, literally all-important. It was a relationship with another human being: something larger than we were, something life-giving.

In an attachment relationship, it's comfortable just to be with that other person, without needing to say anything. When an attachment relationship is severed, even temporarily, there is anxiety and distress. In adulthood, sexual love can extend into attachment, for instance when falling in love becomes love. It's as if the joining with another person in sex can—not always but when we really love someone—be extended to include feelings of contentment, and the desire to nurture the other, to be physically close, to be in a permanent relationship.

In "One Another," the clues are that Alex seems to have a strong attachment relationship with Sonya. He feels comfortable with her. He is anxious when they are apart. However, although for some people sex and attachment are glued firmly together, this seems not to be true for Alex. He has a sexual hankering beyond his attachment relationship with Sonya.

Sometimes, when in a play, novel, or film, an attachment theme is invoked, we can find ourselves in tears. For instance, in *Hamlet* toward the end of the play, Hamlet is fatally wounded in a fencing match in which his opponent Laertes has been fighting with an unbated rapier tipped with poison. As he dies, his friend Horatio says this:

> Now cracks a noble heart. Good night, sweet prince,
> And flights of angels sing thee to thy rest. (5, 2, 364–365).

Following the accumulated meanings of the play up to this point, these words prompt a profound sadness in the audience. Though I have read them many times I still feel tearful when I do so again. How does this effect work? Part of the answer, I think, is in a cognitive process called priming, a kind of induction in which a word or a phase summons up a script or theme in a person's life. "Good night" primes an attachment theme.[3] This phrase invokes the tender scene in which a child is wished good night, reminds us perhaps of such scenes when we were children, or of when we said good night to children of our own. Walt Disney knew this principle and many of his early children's films are about separations and reunions with parents. Very affecting.

We can form attachments, too, to stories, or to an author. Thinking recently about books I read as a child, I remembered reading Arthur Ransome's *Swallows and Amazons* and its sequels. These stories were not as popular in North America as they were in Britain, but you can get the idea if you think of how attached children have become to J.K. Rowling's stories of Harry Potter. In any event, a few weeks before I wrote the paragraph you are now reading, I re-read the first chapter of *Swallows and Amazons*.

The book starts with the seven-year-old Roger, running in wide zigzags up a hill from the shore of a large lake toward where his mother is standing in front of a farm house in which his family is staying for the summer holidays. Instead of running directly toward his mother, which he is tempted to do, because she is holding an envelope in which he thinks, correctly, there is a message from his father for which he and his siblings have been waiting, he continues to run in zigzags. He is a clipper ship tacking against the wind.

As I started to read, I was surprised to find myself in tears, and I continued tearfully to the end of the chapter? Why should this have been? There's nothing sad in the chapter. It is joyous. The message from the children's father, on a ship at Malta bound for Hong Kong, is that the children are allowed to take the small sailing dinghy, *Swallow*, they've found in the farm's boathouse, and sail it to the island about a mile offshore, and camp there.

I don't think my tears came from a sense of loss of a happy childhood. I've had good periods of happiness in my life but, consciously at least, they have mostly been in adulthood.

My tears could perhaps have been nostalgia (defined as memories of things that never happened) but I think they were a matter of attachment, as when one is reunited with an attachment person after a period of separation. In the first paragraph of *Swallows and Amazons*, I was suddenly reunited with an object of attachment: with a book I had read as a child. I read all of Ransome's children's books, I think, when I was between eight and eleven. I used to own the whole set. I remember them on a bookshelf. They must have been given to me, one by one, by my parents.

And—strange that this should only have occurred to me only at this point in my life—at the same time that he planted in me a strong interest in sailing, it must have been Arthur Ransome who gave me my love of fiction. The opening of *Swallows and Amazons* is a perfect example. The prose is transparent. Important elements of fiction are present: the imagination (with Roger as a clipper ship), the shift from exterior to interior (Roger wants to run straight to his mother, but continues his external action of tacking), and the interpersonal (Roger's mother is patient, she knows her son needs to tack toward her, and Roger knows that she knows).

In our studies in which we have asked people to read short stories and to mark Es and Ms in the margin, we have found that reading fiction can prompt memories of autobiographical events. Here, for instance, is a memory that a woman reader experienced when I asked a group of people in a postgraduate course to read the 1894 short story "The Dream of an Hour," by Kate Chopin.

> This sentence about the child crying itself to sleep reminded me of a time when I did [this] myself, when my parents were divorcing. The image struck me as very vivid and brought that day back to me.

The emotion of this memory was sadness, and on a scale of 0 (meaning no emotion at all) to 10 (meaning the most intense emotion of your life) the reader rated its current intensity as 6.

Such memories can get incorporated into our understanding of the story. However, the kind of remembering that occurred to me in re-reading the first chapter of *Swallows and Amazons* wasn't of this kind. My attachment to these children's books was something that I had never thought of consciously. My tears forced me to recognize it. As an extension of this idea, it seems likely that in reading a piece of fiction, something about a setting or an author's style or a character or a situation may find a resonance with some aspect of one's life to which one has an attachment, which can give comfort and connection with the book one is reading.

REFLECTIVE EMOTIONS

If reading for entertainment is based mainly on the pleasure of identification with such figures as heroes and heroines, on ideas of attainment or success, on ideas of love, on anger being revenged, and so on, how do we account for people's interest in stories that end sadly?

Mary Beth Oliver has proposed that, as well as the pleasure-seeking impulse of fictional entertainment, people are also interested in situations that are poignant, that emphasize human vulnerabilities, compassion, and need for emotional support. So as well as the pleasure-seeking impulse and the idea of escape in suspense, she recognizes that people can read to experience emotions that are mixed, and even sad, an experience that she calls "tenderness." Putting this another way, readers and theatergoers are able to approach works of fiction in a way that they appreciate them as works of art, that is to say, as meaningful.

Oliver studied people's responses to films. She found that there were three distinct kinds of response. One was whether the film was fun, one was whether it was suspenseful, and one was whether it was moving and thought provoking. Films that were enjoyed most were those labeled as fun: comedies and romances. Suspense films were not necessarily enjoyed as much as comedies and romances. The films that were most appreciated, however, were those that had longer-lasting effects. Such films offered a distinct kind of gratification. This kind of effect involves not just the emotion one experiences in a play, film, or book, but emotions about these emotions. We could call these reflective emotions, about whether, for instance, one enjoys being able to think about sadness in a particular way, to contemplate and understand new aspects of life.[4]

Holger Schramm and Werner Wirth have done an experiment to take Oliver's idea further. They gave viewers a verbal summary of the first part of Mimi Leder's (2000) film, *Pay It Forward*, and then asked them to watch a clip of the last part of the film. The film is about a young boy, Trevor, whose mother is an alcoholic. One of his teachers gives him a project, to think of something that would change the world. Trevor's idea is that instead of paying back a favor that someone has done, one pays it forward, by doing new good deeds for three other people. Trevor starts to live his idea. It has widening effects, including effects on his mother, and on people he doesn't know. The film is a tragedy because, as he comes to the aid of a classmate who is being assaulted, Trevor is stabbed by the assailant and dies. The researchers made three film-clip versions of the last part of the film. Each clip started with Trevor's birthday party in which a TV journalist interviews him about his project. Then comes the scene in which Trevor is killed. Then there is a scene in which Trevor's mother and his teacher watch the televised interview. Then comes a scene in which hundreds of mourning admirers, all holding candles, come to Trevor's home to honor him. One version of the clip has the film's original score, in which a song "Calling All Angels," is heard over this final scene. The researchers call this version the affective upbeat version, because, although somewhat sad, the song is also optimistic. In a second version—the affective downbeat version—the song is replaced by a neutral piece of instrumental music, Beethoven's *Moonlight Sonata*. In the third version—the cognitive switch version—the original last scene of the film accompanied by music is omitted, and the film clip ends silently with Trevor's mother and teacher watching the televised interview.

The results of the study were that the downbeat version made people most sad, but the cognitive switch version enabled people to enjoy the film most. The authors suggest this occurred because the ending with Trevor talking directly to them in the television interview enabled them to transform their own sad feelings of his death to thinking about the meaning of Trevor's project.

The beginning of cognitive psychology, the kind of psychology on which the discussion parts of this book are based, came with a book called *Remembering*, published by Frederic Bartlett in 1932. It was based principally on English people's rememberings of a Native American folk story they were asked to read. In his book, Bartlett proposed that we are constantly trying to make sense of the world, and for this he coined the phrase "effort after meaning." We make this effort in our everyday lives as we try to understand why a friend said what she said, or why a relative did what he did. We make this effort when we are faced with something unfamiliar, as the English readers of the Native American folk story were faced by a tale from a culture entirely different from their own. We make this effort, too, when we read a piece of print fiction or go to the theater. A good piece of fiction does not just pass the time. It enables and encourages our effort after meaning. The enjoyment of sadness in stories is in the reflection. It does not invite as much fun as in comedies, but often it's more satisfying.

ONE ANOTHER

PART V

Back in London, David was furious.

"How could you be so naive?"

"I'm sorry," said Alex. "I've said I'm sorry. I was in the hands of professionals."

"You had your dick out. Not difficult for anyone to get their hands on it."

Alex bit his lip.

"When you've got one thing to do," said David, "you do that one thing."

"I was naive. I'm incredibly sorry."

"If you want to go out shagging, then go out shagging."

David closed his eyes. He reached his left hand through his hair and over to the back of his head, his face on his upper arm.

"Shit," he said. "Shit."

Alex wondered again why he'd agreed to go and pick the document up in Leningrad. Was it anxiety that the medical project he was working on was too humdrum?

"I'll have another go," said Alex.

"You'll do no such bloody thing."

"I can't bear being taken for a ride."

"You don't mind taking me for a ride."

"That's not it."

"You decided to do your own thing."

"I'll make it up."

"Don't be stupid."

"I'll be your slave. I'll do whatever you want to make it up to you."

"You should look at yourself."

When David got in touch with the dissident to tell him his manuscript had been stolen, he seemed philosophical. He had a copy, but he'd decided the whole book needed reworking. It was never clear whether he thought it needed rewriting because the copy that Alex was to bring back had been lost, or whether he would have decided that anyway. The dissident was still agreeing to do it. It was a matter of time.

For a while David continued to speak to Alex in a grumpy way, but his actions had their usual friendly quality.

"The Vermeer project," said David. "The woman wants to do it. Dead keen, but she's not an easy person, and she's a procrastinator. This time it's your actual job to be Mr Charming."

Alex winced. "What job?" he said.

"Here's the file, with correspondence. I want you to look after the whole project, but I'd prefer you didn't take the file out of the office. Who knows what might happen to it."

David had labeled the file VERMEER, in big black letters. It was in a yellow cardboard folder, and Alex suddenly had the thought that the color was the same as the yellow patch of wall in Vermeer's *View of Delft*, that Proust had his character Bergotte notice.

He took the file, and nodded: "OK."

"Go to Amsterdam" said David. "Tell the woman we'll do all the fiddly things, arrange permissions and so on. In fact that won't be we, it'll be you. But she's got to get on with it."

"I'll do that."

"Set up a timetable. Tell her that you'll read everything she writes, tell her to send it to you and you'll return it within 48 hours with suggestions."

Alex started leafing through the file of typed pages and pictures.

"Her English is good." said David. "Tell her that you'll make it not just perfect, but beautiful. We want a manuscript, and we it now, not in three or four years time."

. . .

It was in May that Sonya and Alex arranged to meet in Warsaw. She had permission to attend a conference and he had been able to get a visa.

Alex had been in a bad state since he'd returned from Leningrad. He knew David felt he'd been a fool. What was it that had made it so easy for Toril to take him in? But it hadn't just been that. What was worse was to have glimpsed something with her. Why wasn't the reality of Sonya more real than Toril's subterfuge? Was there some fundamental problem, deep inside him? He consulted a friend and decided to enter psychotherapy. He was determined to change.

Alex arrived in Warsaw a day before Sonya was due. He'd reserved a room in a hotel near the center of the city. The room looked out on the Soviet-built Palace of Culture, the most prominent building in Warsaw. In London he'd heard the joke about the building: the best views of the city are from its upper floors because from there you can't see it.

Alex had missed Sonya terribly, wanted desperately to make it work during the time they would spend together. The evening after he'd arrived, he reconnoitered the neighborhood for a restaurant to which he could take Sonya to lunch next day when he brought her back from the airport. He chose one, went in to have supper, found fault with it, and came back to the hotel discouraged. Next day, he went to the airport and arrived half an hour before her plane was due. He was agitated. When at last he saw her approach, he smiled with delight. He felt very weak. He held on to her. Sonya was surprised to find him in tears.

"Whatever is it?" she said.

"I'm all right. I'm sorry. I'm being silly."

"No need to be sorry." She held him close, feeling something of his tearfulness. "It's all right, I'm here."

"I'm sorry," he said. "I've been looking forward to seeing you."

Alex recovered himself and took Sonya's suitcase.

"How was the flight?" he said. "The hotel's passable, near the center."

They went to the hotel to drop off Sonya's things, went to lunch in a restaurant that seemed to Alex no better than the one he'd eaten in the night before. They walked around the center of the town, holding hands. It would be all right. Why ever had he had any doubts?

Alex felt he'd learned from the episode with Toril. That was its real importance. Not being duped, not the anger, not the disappointment. He'd learned about himself, learned what was important. It was Sonya. She was a proper person, with a real mother, a real life. There were real problems to solve. It was her he cared about. He knew that. His doubts and hesitations had been ridiculous.

They went to bed early that evening and made love. Alex lay on his back, and an image of Toril came into his mind.

"Could you come over here, for a little while," he said. "Sit on top of me, and hover a bit."

"Like this?"

Next day, Sonya went to her conference. It was an important conference, and she was pleased to have been invited. Alex sensed in her a new confidence. He took a tram to the Old Town, which had been bombed into nothingness in the war and had been rebuilt brick-by-brick to reproduce all the streets, all the buildings, all the lampposts, exactly as it had been. Alex had read that one of the guides to the reconstruction was a set of paintings that Canaletto had done of the Old Town. Life now imitated art.

Toril came back into his mind. He dismissed her immediately. It's just a pattern of sensation, he thought. With Sonya, it's about her, the real her.

Alex and Sonya had a week together. It seemed almost perfect, one of the closest times they had spent.

"Not the town," she said. "Just being here. Lovely. I love my mother, but sometimes she gets me down."

"Being here together."

"If only we could do it more often."

"Or all the time."

"Exactly."

"When I go to Moscow," she said, "it seems like a step toward the East. Warsaw seems like a step toward the West. I miss that time in London."

"Everything's changing," he said. "Here in Poland things are changing a lot. Solidarność, the election coming up. They might win."

"In Leningrad it's not clear what's happening."

.   .   .

Two years after Alex had gone to Leningrad to fetch the manuscript, the dissident had finished rewriting his book, and huge changes were occurring in the Soviet Union. Someone else went to collect the manuscript and had no trouble. Perhaps the Soviet authorities had other things to think about. By the time the book had been translated, the USSR was no more.

The dissident's book was every bit as good as Alex had anticipated. It was a story of a Russian man and an American woman, each channeled by an upbringing, each too caught up in an ideology, each too focused on a vision of the future to be able to care properly for each other in the day-to-day. It was an allegory. In his foreword to the book, Alex told the story of the dissident and his literary distinction, of his troubles with the authorities. He told, too, the story of his own journey to Leningrad in 1988, of his picking up the manuscript from a dank basement in the Liteyniy district, of taking the train from the Finland Station, of being hit in the back with a rifle butt at the border.

As Alex wrote his foreword, he reflected on how the Soviet system had crumbled because although Stalin's cruelties were past, it managed—despite its aspirations to foster equality—to reduce the life of too many of its citizens to a daily grind. The idea of a system that knew better than its individuals how each one should live may have been alright in medieval times, but no longer. He thought of Toril's assignment to seduce him and steal the manuscript as a symptom. But what about inequality? He put that thought aside for another time. The system! He'd not been able to confront it himself, but its coming to an end induced a certain satisfaction.

In his foreword, Alex described how, in his hotel room in Helsinki, he'd taken out the manuscript and looked at it, and stowed it back in his rucksack, with his clothes carefully beside it. He mentioned the fact that he had gone to the bar for a glass of fruit juice before going to bed and that, next morning, when he went to get a clean shirt from his rucksack, the envelope with the manuscript in it was no longer there. Certain other facts of the evening at Hotel Seurahuone were omitted.

Alex wrote of the dissident's insistence on rewriting the manuscript. He discussed the book's literary and historical importance, and said that even though the Soviet system was no more, the book had profound implications for society as a whole.

The book made a stir, but it was a milder stir than would have occurred if Alex had managed to bring the manuscript back when he'd gone for it.

Chapter 5

Transformation

Stories tend to start with one or more characters in a certain emotional state, which is then disrupted. As a result, changes occur. In some stories, they occur in the inner lives of characters who reach a new emotional state by the end of the story. Changes can also occur in us as readers.

A five-year-old girl picks up a banana and holds it to her ear. "Hello," she says. "Can I talk to Emily, please." A banana has become a telephone. We call this symbolic play. It's uniquely human. Play is the very emblem of enjoyment, of doing something for its own sake. The processes that underlie it are also the psychological bases of art. The center of art is the creation of a that from a this.

For years, we have been told that our ancestors made knives and scrapers from stone: useful things. Only recently has discussion begun of other kinds of objects in the archaeological record: objects that are not practical but symbolic. They include objects of art, which are both themselves and something else.

As well as objects, one's own self can undergo transformation because, in both play and in a story, a person can remain himself or herself and also become someone else. In literary theory, this is called identification. By Part V of "One Another" a change has occurred to Alex. For the most part, the reader keeps his or her own thoughts and feelings, but if he or she has taken some of the concerns on of Alex and Sonya, there's a possibility of a change of selfhood in the reader, too.

THE ARCHAEOLOGY OF ART

The earliest known objects of art in the archaeological record are shells in which holes were drilled 82,000 years ago to make beads that could be worn in strings as necklaces. They were discovered recently in the area that is now Morocco. In the area that is now Slovenia, a flute has been found that is 43,000 years old. In the area that is now Australia, evidence of ritual burial has been found from about 40,000 years ago. In an area that is now France, the earliest cave paintings, 31,000 years old, were discovered.[1]

Steven Mithen has proposed that finds of this sort suggest that, at some time in the last 100,000 years, an important evolutionary change occurred in the human mind. Before this, he says, people were knowledgeable, but their knowledge was confined to specific domains, such as knowledge of others in the social group, knowledge of foodstuffs, knowledge of the immediate geographical region. Each kind of knowledge was limited to one domain. Mental life is still very affected by this kind of partitioning: knowing how to ride a bicycle is no help in learning algebra.

Findings such as the ancient beads, the flute, the burial sites, the cave paintings suggest—says Mithen—that some domains of knowledge began to interpenetrate. A this could be a that! Metaphor was born. A shell was not just a shell. It was a bead. A piece of wood was also a musical instrument. A dead person was alive on another plane. Charcoal marks on a cave wall were a rhinoceros.

So, at a relatively recent stage of our evolution, we humans became art-making beings. Language, which may have emerged

200,000 years ago,[2] already had some of this property, since something said is both a sound and what it means. Stories extend the symbolic property. Sounds and words can become the abstractions of character and action in stories. Although humans have, for a long time, been able to think, and even to know that they were thinking, it seems possible that, with the advent of stories, they became able to think about such symbolic figures as ancestors and heroes, then able to think in a more conscious way about others and themselves.

Long after the first archaeological signs of art were made, writing was invented, just 5,000 years ago, and was able to transcend the ephemeral in a new way. With it came metaphor in the literary sense. As humankind moved from prehistory to history, from the entirely oral to the partly literate, Sappho would write: "Love makes me tremble again...sweet-bitter creature."[3]

In his recent and fascinating book on the novel, Nobel Prize–winning novelist Orhan Pamuk devotes his second chapter to this issue: How is it that we know that fiction is imaginary and can also seem real? Talking about his novel *The Museum of Innocence*, he says:

> I intended my novel to be perceived as a work of the imagination—yet I also wanted readers to assume that the main characters and the story were true...I have learned that the art of writing is to feel these contradictory desires deeply (p. 34).

METAPHOR AND SELFHOOD

A central experience of fiction is the one in which characters depicted in words become people in our minds, people whom we know. The more important part, however, is that, because fiction's transactions are in the realm of the symbolic, fiction can affect us personally. It can enable a jog from the this of our current self toward the that of a possible self. When we read, we are both our own everyday self and, as we enter into fictional lives and situations of a story, we can take on aspects of someone who has a relationship with a character or, in identification, even take aspects of a character into our selves. For the most part, this is temporary. But residues can remain, and over time our selfhood can change.

This ability to transform the self by entering imaginary worlds starts in childhood. When the five-year-old girl uses a banana as a telephone, it's not just the banana that is transformed, it's the girl herself. From being a five-year-old, she becomes an adult who has the technical skills to phone her friend.

Children's play gives us a glimpse of some of the properties of fiction. To play means to be able to take part in a piece of interaction both as oneself and as someone else. So, to play at being a shopkeeper, a child is both him- or herself and also a shopkeeper. In "One Another," as we identify with Alex, we are ourselves and him.

Now, a person can sit in Toronto or London and mentally enter a situation in Tokyo or Lahore. Or, as in Leo Tolstoy's short story "Kholstomer," a person can experience what it might be like to be a horse. Or the person can experience being just one human being among the billions who have lived, and have a sense of an emotion of the whole of humankind. Readers can transform themselves by metaphor.

This is somewhat like being an actor who is him- or herself and also a character in a theatrical role, and—like actors—we as readers can bring a story alive. In our trajectories through stories, as we meet other characters, we experience the emotions that we would experience in following the desires of those characters.

We feel emotions as we re-experience memories from our own lives, and as we experience certain scriptlike sequences that are meaningful to humankind. And again, we experience these emotions in ourselves.

In chapter 3, I introduced Freud's paper on the question of where the creative writer gets his or her ideas. Freud's answer was that the writer indulges in play in a fashion that is similar to that of childhood, to pursue wishes. In childhood, says Freud, play tends to have an underlying wish, to be a grown up. In the same kind of way, he says, as adults we often wish to be someone different, someone who achieves something remarkable. Freud proposed that writers, especially popular writers, offer stories that are expressions of such wishes.

Just as when we were children, we knew, if we were playing a chase-game in the playground at school that, if we were caught we would not be killed, so in a story in which the protagonist is in danger, we know it's the confronting of the danger that is the thing, because through it a wished-for state of accomplishment might be attained.

Just as in childhood, play is a source of pleasure so, in adulthood, fiction is a source of pleasure. What do people like to do when they have time to themselves? They often like to spend this time in entertainment, a kind of play. In the course of our lives, says Freud, we don't generally give up our pleasures. Instead we tend to change the ways in which we take part in them. Although chase-games diminish toward the end of childhood, these activities are exchanged for fiction and sports that derive from the same sources. In them, we can be a protagonist battling against odds, we can identify with a particular sports team or take an interest in a particular athlete. As someone who identifies with a protagonist in a heroic story or who is a supporter of a team or an athlete who triumphs, we take pleasure in success without endangering our health, and, in the case of sports, without the repetitiveness of training or the pain of effort.

Freud had started to think of the connection between literature and play several years before he wrote his article on creative writers. In an article of 1905–1906, he wrote that being a member of an audience at the theatre:

> ...does for adults what play does for children... The spectator...is a "poor wretch to whom nothing of importance can happen," who has long been obliged to damp down, or rather displace, his ambition to stand at the hub of world affairs; he longs to feel and to act and to arrange things according to his own desires—in short, to be a hero. And the playwright and actor enable him to do this by allowing him *to identify himself* with the hero (p. 122, emphasis in original).

Some people find Freud's theories preposterous. You might nonetheless find this theory about literary art and aspiration worthwhile, even if you are generally skeptical of Freud's ideas. Without some notion of fiction being based on a certain kind of playlike fantasy, it is difficult to understand its appeal. And, if you are worried about the preposterous, think of the provocatively dressed vamps and gun-toting tough guys who routinely prance across our film and television screens.

When we are in a play world, this world needs to be self-consistent. It's thought by some that children can be so caught up in their imagination that they cannot distinguish truth from imagination. This is not true. Research by Paul Harris[4] shows that children can understand characteristics of an imaginary world perfectly well, and they can know that such characteristics are separate from those of the ordinary world. If some children are playing at having a tea party, and an adult knocks over a cup, spills some pretend tea, makes a show of wiping it up, and asks a child to pour some more tea, the child knows to pour pretend tea from the toy teapot into just that cup that was knocked over. The child does not pour pretend tea into any of the other cups, which, like that one, also contain nothing but air.

A writer, too, has to keep the imagined world of a story consistent, otherwise people feel he or she isn't playing the game. Writers of detective stories can use the idea of inconsistencies, so that a clever detective will notice them. One of the best detectives in English fiction is E.C. Bentley's Philip Trent and, in the first story of *Trent Intervenes*, a perpetrator makes a mistake of thinking that All Souls College, at Oxford, has undergraduates in the same way as do other Oxford Colleges. In the real world, it's not so, and in the imagined world of the story, the mistake leads Trent to suspect a confidence trick. He turns out to be right.

Consistency within imagined worlds and consistency of these worlds with what we know of the real world are evidently important in fiction. In detective fiction, there is often a succession of patterns that seem to fit the facts that the reader is invited to consider. Patterns that are introduced at the beginning of the story contain inconsistencies that the detective spots until, by the story's end, the detective will disclose the final answer, a pattern of interpretation of what lies beneath surface appearances—the deep pattern—which is convincing because it is without inconsistencies.

CHANGE IN SELFHOOD

In ordinary life, each emotion that we experience signals a change in our outer world or in our inner world, a change that affects something we value, a change that may perhaps cause some transformation of our self. Usually, the change is tiny but, for some emotional events, such as falling in love or the threat of violence, it can be immense.

"One Another" is set at a time when huge changes began to occur in the Soviet Union and countries of the Eastern Bloc like Poland.[5] The changes enabled Alex and Sonya to spend some time together, and to start to think about changes of their own, such as whether they should live with each other.

Emotions of fictional characters occur because of events in the story world. As in the day-to-day world, they occur when such events affect a concern and indicate that, in relation to it, things are going better or worse than expected. Changes of plan are required, changes of relationship, changes of the self.

By part V of "One Another," changes have started to occur in Alex. His selfhood, which he has not understood all that well, has been challenged by the performance that Toril put on for him as if she were playing a part in a theater. He is sufficiently troubled by its effects, and by the lack of self-understanding that it indicated, that he enters psychotherapy. At the same time he has an aspiration, an ideal self, to become someone who is able to commit himself to Sonya. It's toward this ideal self that he wants to move. If we identify with Alex as we read, we can remain ourselves and at the same time extend ourselves into his ideas, into something like his state in the story.

In part III of "One Another," it was not just himself whom Alex let down. By his liaison with Toril, he let down Sonya. Although he keeps this from Sonya, he doesn't keep it from David, the friend who has looked after him, who made sure to get him a new job, and who gave him the commission of picking up the dissident's manuscript. David is angry. Because he is fond of Alex, David doesn't end their relationship, but he demands that Alex should change. Alex promises to do so, and they make up.

Aristotle thought that change is essential to a story. Each story, he says, has a beginning, a middle, and an end. The beginning usually has two aspects: to introduce the characters, who've been going along in their lives in a more or less stable way, and to depict an event that destabilizes the characters or their situation. For Alex, the destabilization is his commission to smuggle a manuscript out of the USSR. The middle part of a story includes what Aristotle called a *peripeteia*, a large change, a main turning point. The end of a story is a resolution. Questions of the earlier parts have to be answered: What will the repercussions of this *peripeteia* be?

I think of short stories as related to sonnets. Not only are they short, but there are several constraints. The sonnet form has 14 lines, a particular meter (iambic pentameter), and a particular rhyming scheme. This form, then, offers constraints to the writer. Most importantly, in the commonest sonnet form (the Petrarchan form), there is a constraint related to meaning. It is that between line 8 and line 9 there should be a turning point that corresponds to a *peripeteia*. In "One Another," such a turning point occurs between part III, in the hotel room in Helsinki, and part IV when Alex discovers the loss of the manuscript. Alex's forward movement is stopped; everything seems to go into reverse.

As well as enjoying the structuring required by this constraint of the *peripeteia*, in writing "One Another," I have also rather enjoyed being responsive to constraints of moving through a range of emotions. It's been interesting for me—and it has affected the story—to be responsive to these constraints, and it's changed the way I have written: going back and forth between the story and the discussion sections of the book.

As I mentioned in the previous section, it's not just characters who change in fiction. Much more importantly, by entering into a piece of fiction, we, as readers, can experience changes in ourselves. In an experiment, Maja Djikic, Sara Zoeterman, Jordan Peterson, and I asked whether reading a short story could contribute to a change in readers' personalities. We randomly assigned 166 people to read either a literary short story or a version of the story in a nonfiction format that described all its events. Before and after people read either the story or the nonfiction styled version, we measured their personalities using a standard personality inventory. Also, in the manner I described in chapter 4, we measured readers' emotions, by giving them a list of emotion terms and asking them to say how intensely they felt each emotion, before reading and again after reading.

The literary story was "The Lady with the Toy Dog," by Anton Chekhov. This is generally acknowledged to be one of the world's great short stories. It begins at a seaside resort, Yalta, and it's about Dmitri Gomov and Anna Sergueyevna. They are both alone, on vacation. The story starts with Gomov noticing Anna as she walks her little dog. Both Gomov and Anna are married to other people. They begin an affair. At the end of their vacation they part, but, instead of fading pleasantly, their feelings for each other grow, and each is shocked to discover how much more important these feelings are than anything else in their lives. The change that occurs for Gomov is that from being self-absorbed, a man disappointed in his work and his marriage, a philanderer, he comes to be totally absorbed with Anna, and feels generously toward her. Both Gomov and Anna have commitments. The story ends with this: "...their hardest and most difficult period was only just beginning."

Maja Djikic wrote the nonfiction styled version to include all the events of Chekhov's story as a courtroom report of divorce proceedings. We arranged this version carefully to have the same characters, the same events, even many of the words of Chekhov's story. It was exactly the same length and reading difficulty. When we gave it to the readers in our study, they found it just as interesting, though not as artistic, as Chekhov's story. The difference was in the art of Chekhov's fiction.

The results of our study were that the personality traits of people who read Chekhov's story changed more than did those of the people who read the courtroom account. The changes in personality were not large, but they were measurable.

As I discussed in chapter 2, the best fiction does not deal with beliefs but with thoughts. In "The Lady with the Toy Dog," there is no attempt by the writer to be persuasive. The changes of personality that we measured in the readers of Chekhov's story were all in different directions. Each one was individual to the particular reader: each person changed in his or her own way. The changes in personality that occurred, moreover, were such that the more intense their emotions while reading, the more people changed in their personality.

We think that readers' changes in personality were due to the art of Chekhov's story taking people out of themselves. These changes were also affected by experiencing emotions of empathy with the protagonists. That is to say, some readers identified with Gomov or Anna or both, each in his or her own way, so that some became a bit more like one of the characters. Probably, too, acting as moral monitors, some readers disapproved of how Gomov and Anna thought and acted. Each in their own way, the readers of the story found themselves involved in it so that they began to change how they thought and felt about themselves.

We did another analysis of our results on the people who read Chekhov's story or the nonfiction-styled divorce-court version. We measured readers' styles of attachment to other people. (Remember the idea of attachment from chapter 4.) We identified those who were avoidant, that is to say those who anxiously tended to avoid close commitments, who tended to overdistance their emotions so that they would not feel anything too much. We found that readers who scored high on avoidance and who were in the group that read Chekhov's story rather than the nonfiction-styled text, had larger changes in emotion as they read the story than did those who were not avoidant. Chekhov's story enabled people who habitually clamped down their emotions to feel more intensely than they usually did. The nonfiction-styled version did not have this effect. So literary art was able to find its way around the usual defensiveness of the avoidant people. The story was a safe way for them to be able to experience emotions.

One of the functions of fiction is to invite people into an identification, to empathize and sympathize with the characters, to prompt in them ideas of themselves at remembered moments in their lives, to take part in universal emotional patterns, or to follow trails of curiosity, but not in any prescribed way. Fiction is not persuasion. In the better kinds of fiction, the author doesn't try to make you feel in some particular way or to believe any particular thing. However, I think, just as changes can occur for characters in a story—in the way that Gomov becomes less self-centered and more concerned for Anna—so changes of selfhood can occur to us as we read, changes that are not programmed or coerced but that are individual and self-chosen. In our research, we inferred that the nonfiction format of the proceedings of a divorce court were less inviting of empathy, sympathy, the promptings of memory, universal emotional patterns, and curiosity, and were less inviting to personal change.

Another recent study that found effects of personal change with fiction was by Marc Sestir and Melanie Green. They had viewers watch one of four movie clips from commercial films, each centered on a particular character. Some viewers were given instructions to identify, "as if you were the main character in the clip," whereas others were asked to watch "as if you were an independent observer of the narrative." In a task that accessed the viewers' sense of their own personality, participants who were asked to identify with the movie character (but not those asked to watch the film as independent observers) were found to change by taking on some of the movie character's traits.[6]

With a single story, any changes that occur in one's sense of self are usually small and temporary. What may happen with the reading of a lot of fiction, however, is that they can accumulate, and the reader can become more flexible.[7] Are you, the reader of this book, likely to change as a result of reading "One Another?" It will depend on how well, from your point of view, I have written the story, how intense your emotions are as you read it, whether you identify with Alex or Sonya, and whether the story touches something in you that you might want to change.

HOW DO WE CHANGE?

How do we change in our everyday lives? We may set out to give up smoking, to give up lingering anger toward another person, or to take up mindfulness practice, and there are famous accounts of religious conversions.[8] However, for most of us, the most profound and lasting changes occur as a result of entering relationships with others. We fall in love. We become a parent. We start a job with responsibilities to others. We become sick or disabled so that we need care from others. We are victims of civil or military violence. Such occurrences are called life events, and they can change us in substantial ways.[9]

Fiction distills such changes into a set that may not yet have happened to us, but that are presented in a way that we can feel and think about them, so that we can experience some flavor of them before they occur in our lives. Although fiction is not without encounters with volcanoes or effects of sea voyages, for the most part, the encounters of a protagonist are with other fictional characters, some of whom are allies who affect the protagonist for the better, and some of whom are antagonists who oppose the protagonist.

Just as in day-to-day life, we are affected by others as we engage in fiction. The effects on ourselves arise from characters, from how we think of them as people.

As Dolf Zillmann has proposed, we closely monitor the morality of characters in fiction. We judge whether they behave well or badly. In the same kind of way we observe our friends in what they do and how they do it, in how they feel about what they do, in how they affect others. We also monitor ourselves, though not always as harshly as when we judge others. When we share an emotion with someone else,[10] it's as if we can catch a glimpse of ourselves in the mirror of conversation. Fiction offers a wider set of mirrors than those usually available to us.

Emotions are important in fiction for the same reason that they are important in our everyday lives. They signal changes to the world in which we are engaged. They are the bases of our values. They give us our sense of ourselves. Our social lives are full of emotion: of love, of anger, of liking that is not-quite love, of shame, of envy, of contempt, and so on. Fiction offers us characters who are affected by their emotions. With them, and for them, we feel emotions that are comparable to those of our lives.

Just as when we take part in a conversation, we talk about our own and others' plans, events, and emotions, so in fiction we think about events of the emotional kind. We think about them in a world of imagination in which we may sometimes come to more or different realizations than we do in ordinary life. These realizations can complement those of ordinary life. Sometimes they are less profound, but sometimes they can be more profound and change us.

ONE ANOTHER

PART VI

The phone rang.

"A woman to see you," said the receptionist who was stationed at the front desk.

Alex was in his office at the publishing house. He was thinking he'd leave in a few minutes and walk over to David's office to work there during the afternoon. The Vermeer project was coming to fruition, and the book looked terrific. One of the best parts was a chapter that compared the artist's vision with the idea of the photographic *camera obscura* that Vermeer used to trace his perspectives. Then this part made comparisons of Vermeer's original paintings with the forgeries of van Meegeren, and with reproductions such as those in the book. Alex had worked very closely with the writer in her discussion of the relation between what was on the retina and what was in the mind of a viewer. The writer had had some really good ideas, but the chapter had been something of a collaboration. It was better than anything he knew on this topic.

"I'm not expecting anyone," said Alex to the receptionist. "Who is it?"

"Toril Ericsson."

It was a shock. He'd not thought of her for a week, maybe two weeks.

"I'll come to the front," he said.

There she was. Her bent nose and her face were still attractive, but here in the waiting area that publishers have by the reception desk, she looked somehow dowdy.

The receptionist was watching. Alex shook Toril's hand, rather formally.

"Shall we go out," he said. "It gets a bit stuffy in here."

He nodded toward the receptionist. They walked out, into The Strand.

"Aren't you going to kiss me?" she said. "Or you're still too angry."

"Wouldn't you be angry?"

"I thought you would understand, or I wouldn't have tracked you down. Do you have any idea what they're capable of?"

"You mean were capable of? Isn't that why you're here?"

"I saw the book had come out. I wanted to see you," she said.

"Do you want a coffee?"

"Why not?"

They went to a small coffee shop that was not crowded.

Alex's thoughts raced. What to say? Be on the cool side. See how things unfold.

They went to the counter. She asked for a Cappuccino. Normally he would have had one too. Instead he ordered an Americano. They waited silently for the coffees to be made. Alex's thoughts raced.

"Aren't you pleased to see me, just a little bit?" she said when they sat down.

"You weren't you. You were someone else."

She picked up the little spoon that coffee shops provide, and stirred some of the froth of her Cappuccino into the liquid.

"You're not Swedish," he said. "You were with the KGB."

"You think I was doing it for fun?"

"It wasn't that they were holding your mother and father, and would torture them?"

"They had your whole life. Everything."

"Was it just you in the hotel? Or did you have someone with you, who took you back to Leningrad by car."

"Just me. I went to the station, waited out of sight on the platform, watched to see if you came at the last moment, then I got on the train."

"To save us from ourselves?"

"I've come to see you," she said. "I wanted to see you."

Saying this seemed difficult for her. She looked anguished and, of a sudden, Alex felt for her.

"Something happened between us," she said. "I haven't been able to stop thinking about you."

"Why didn't you leave a note? Three words would have been enough."

"I'm sorry."

They were both silent for several minutes.

"Give me a chance," she said. "It's not something I wanted to do. It's been awful for me. You touched me, very deeply. I keep thinking about it. Thinking about you."

She looked into Alex's eyes, appealingly. He returned her look. If he could see in there, he thought, what would it be like?

"I need your help," she said. "I've left Russia. I've come here. Russian rubles aren't worth anything, not that I ever had many."

"You're a computer programmer?"

"I don't know one end of a computer from another."

"But you've got skills?"

"I speak Swedish, and some English. I haven't been to university."

"They trained you?"

"I was an actress. I wasn't a success. I was very upset about that. Then they recruited me."

"Why have you come here?"

She didn't reply. Instead she looked into his eyes again.

· · · ·

They made an arrangement to meet three hours later. He didn't know what to do. Some part of her, that he had taken to when they had first met, was still there. He sensed it in her: her warmth, her smile. He remembered her affection. Was that the actress or the real person? She could not have been more affectionate. Perhaps this was a second chance.

When they met at six o'clock, they went to a hotel. Another impulse? He wasn't going to risk taking her to his house.

In the hotel room, they undressed each other, and were soon in bed. She had the same beautiful body. It wasn't long before he felt moved by being close to her. Her hands were at the back of his neck, on his chest, everywhere.

"What would you like?" she said. "Would you like me to come over here? On top of you?"

It was what he would like, and he did like it. But it wasn't the same. Not at all the same.

When they'd finished, he said: "Shall we go and have something to eat?"

"That would be very nice."

They walked to a Szechuan restaurant he knew. Toril seemed freed up by love making, and was chattering.

"We do have something. That time is past. The Soviet Union is yesterday. This is today."

She grasped him by the arm as they walked along.

"I don't want to pressure you," she said. "Maybe it will work out between us, maybe it won't. But we do have something. You know we do. We should give it a chance. I know I was horrible. But I'll make it up to you. Completely. If I could stay with you for a little while. We could see how things work out. I'll be completely devoted. I can be good for you. We'll have the most wonderful sex you can imagine."

As they sat in the restaurant, Alex had a sudden thought of those Russian women who advertised themselves as partners for Western businessmen. Life-long soul mates. He felt suddenly alarmed—his recoil was almost physical—with that sense he had never been able bear in women: the cloying, the solicitous, the dependent.

Involuntarily, Alex had a thought of Sonya, of his irritation when he sensed her as too dependent. A thought flashed that his sexual difficulties with her arose because of this sense.

Alex looked across the table at Toril. Not having a purpose in life, they make it their purpose to get a man, he thought. They glom onto him. Toril was still studying the menu. Alex was angry now. He clenched his jaw. She'd taken him for a ride once. One time too many. Now she's been dumped by the KGB, and she thinks: "Why not try again?" The same theater but a different scene: needy and pleading.

He ordered for both of them. They didn't say much until the food had been eaten.

"This was fun," she said. "I haven't had that kind of food. See what fun we can have."

"Look," he said. "I've got to go now. I've got a guest coming this evening."

To make the point, he glanced at his watch.

"He's due quite soon, so I've got to be home. You stay in the hotel. I've paid for the room. Tomorrow morning, eight o'clock sharp, I'll phone you. We'll make arrangements."

At 8 o'clock in the morning, Alex imagined Toril in the hotel bedroom, with her hair combed, wearing high-heeled shoes, dressed carefully to look quite the catch, sitting on the side of the bed, waiting for the phone to ring.

Alex didn't phone. He didn't ever talk to Toril again. During the next hour and the rest of that day, and in the days thereafter, he wondered if he had done the right thing.

Chapter 6

Anger and Retribution

Stories of anger involve an expectation that has been breached, in which a person's status and selfhood are demeaned. Anger signals a wrong that demands to be righted, a readjustment that needs to be made in a relationship. Readers can easily feel angry on behalf of a protagonist who has been victimized, who may follow an urge to exact retribution.

Although, worldwide, love is the most common subject of stories, close behind is anger.[1] A typical anger story from world literature is of two brothers. One is a rightful heir, but the other displaces him and sends him into exile. The brother in exile does noteworthy deeds and returns to fight the usurping brother in a battle that is long, cruel, and bloody. Finally the rightful heir takes his rightful place. In Europe there's a related form called the revenge tragedy, in which a benign king is secretly killed. The king's son then plans revenge against the murderer who mounts counterplots that lead to an eruption of violence in which both the murderer and the avenger are killed. Shakespeare's *Hamlet* is an adaptation of this idea.

Stripped-down versions of anger themes occur in thrillers and adventure stories, with a protagonist who is attacked or victimized, and enters a conflict with the antagonist to take revenge.

In fiction, the conflict between a protagonist and an antagonist is often dramatized into physical combat, which may draw out into a long battle, and which often portrays the protagonist acting in a way that is as heinous as that of the perpetrator. We seem easily able to respond to this kind of story. The conflict takes on the character of a moral struggle between right and wrong. It's as if the antagonist comes to represent what is wrong in the world, which needs at any cost—any cost!—to be not just overcome but demolished. An eye-for-an-eye seems embedded in our psyche so deeply that, beneath it, there can often be a cost in inner moral corruption of wanting to exact two eyes for an eye.

When, in "One Another" Toril returns, Alex thinks of her as the antagonist who has deceived him and embodied what is wrong in the world, a wrongness that, of course, needs to be demolished. However, was it really Toril who humiliated him, or was it the Soviet system against which he pitted himself by trying to smuggle the manuscript? Might the Soviets have had their own reasons for wanting to act as they did? And was not Toril a pawn, acting in way that might not be difficult to understand?

STATUS AND SHAME

One of the facts of human life is that we live in hierarchies of status. Status means power. The status of parents is superior to that of offspring, the status of employers is superior to that of employees, the status of the rich is superior to that of the poor, and so on. Although people of higher status often have a duty to care for those of lower status, as parents do for children and teachers do for students, and although, perhaps surprisingly, we are good at living peaceably with people of different status than ourselves, we seem especially attuned to losses of status. We can lose status in many ways, by being betrayed, by being harshly criticized, by being shamed. A frequent result is anger, which can be seen as a move to reassert, or regain, status.

Stories of status, anger, and revenge draw from a deep well of human psychology, supported by biology and by many, though not all, cultures.[2] A hurt or a shame is experienced as a deep wound—a penetration of one's very being—and it is as if our psychological equilibrium can only be regained by inflicting, by means of a carefully executed plan, a comparably penetrating wound.

There are several complications. The first, as pointed out by Arlene Stillwell and her colleagues, is that what seems equitable to an avenger is seldom seen in the same way by the person on whom vengeance is enacted. A second is that, in many societies, the taking of revenge personally is thought to be best replaced by justice enacted with due process by society. A third is that vengefulness can draw not just on an immediate hurt but on a repository of hurt that extends back to childhood. Perhaps, this is because many of us have, from our past, a reservoir of wronged or humiliated feelings. Perhaps it's simply that, as children, we were inevitably of a status that was low and vulnerable to being lowered yet further. Thus, as with stories of romantic love, even for those whose lives are fulfilled, we are not free of our childhood. At least we are not free of childlike longings. So, in stories of being shamed or victimized, certain childhood experiences enable us to resonate with the bitterness of a protagonist, which sets off the desire, as we follow along with a story, for the perpetrator to be pursued and punished.

Psychologists have found that displacement of anger from an original cause to an alternative target is common. Leonard Berkowitz, for instance, has shown that if one imposes any nasty experience on a person—pain, hunger, humiliation, anxiety, insult—that person will feel angry and take it out on whomever may be conveniently at hand. In the person who feels angry, the feelings are likely to include injustice, blame, an urge to punish. Once anger begins, a gathering of thoughts and feelings make the angry person ready to act with aggression, and it's by this means that the person seeks to raise him- or herself in status that has been diminished, and to lower the status of someone else. Berkowitz has done a number of studies of this effect. In one experiment,[3] female students were made to experience pain by holding their arms in cold water. For comparison, other students held their arms in warm water, which was not painful. Those in pain were less likely to reward, and more likely to punish, another student in the experiment whom they knew had nothing to do with inflicting the pain.

As readers, the effects we experience with stories of anger and retribution may be powerful because they resonate with accumulated resentments from our earlier life. Very often, it's unsuitable or impossible to confront perpetrators of childhood harm or humiliation. We can then, as Berkowitz showed, feel propelled to take out anger on some other person or group, nearer at hand and easier to attack. Displaced targets can become psychological equivalents of original perpetrators and, indeed, the phenomenon of displacement can occur in most of us as readers or watchers of stories when we can find ourselves angry at fictional antagonists who are, after all, abstract beings. In stories, vengeful actions can be played out in scenarios of social legitimacy, such as those of a law-enforcement agency or its equivalent. Our role as moral monitors and arbiters is invoked, and inner emotions of anger and punishment can come into effect with all the justification of social legitimacy.

Ideally, one might think that reading or watching stories of anger would heighten our sense of being involved in dynamics of punishment and retribution, and that it would enable us to become more conscious of our inner emotions and desires and their displacements in scenarios of this kind. Often, however, it seems the satisfaction of mentally enacting sequences in which guns blaze and bad guys die, or in which criminals are thrown into jail, is entirely sufficient. We can come away from a book or film based on such a script feeling pleased. Indeed, for some people, the induction of this set of feelings may be even more elemental. Certain kinds of thrillers and action stories seem to depend more strongly on their scenes of violent aggression than on anything in the story line. Violent scenes, in themselves, can become attractive, even addictive, to some people in much the same way as can scenes of pornography.

It's been said that Hollywood's contributions to the movies were cowboys and gangsters—men with guns. Of course, guns have come to signify violence both in the movies and in print stories. In "One Another," I seem to have been unable to forego this trope. In the story, border guards appear with guns, one of which is used to pound Alex in the back. Guns have a symbolic use in stories. In a play, as Chekhov said: "If in the first act you have hung a pistol on the wall, then in the following one it should be fired. Otherwise don't put it there."[4] However, a gun does not just symbolize the possibility of violence. However insignificant the character is, with a gun he or she must be taken notice of.

In "One Another," the theme of the protagonist pitting his wits against a large and impenetrable system is invoked by the setting of the story and by David and Alex's desire to smuggle to the West a document that the Soviet authorities would prohibit. In part IV of the story, the antagonist is personified in Toril. Although the border guards who take Alex off the train at Vyborg are the first visible representations of the antagonist, as characters they are indistinct. Toril is more palpable, someone we come to know to some extent.

As anger grows in Alex, we recognize from within ourselves that he wants retribution, but with a system as vast as the Soviet Union, the possibility of finding Toril is remote. So, in this story, the forward thinking of anger is blocked when Alex finds Toril had stolen the manuscript, and the story suggests that it's at this point that he becomes sad.

The backward-thinking influence of sadness prompts Alex to reflect on his own role in bringing about the state of affairs he is in, having been duped and having his mission to bring back the dissident's manuscript brought to nothing. When he first met Toril and made love with her, he had a fleeting thought of Sonya, and we can wonder how his thoughts of his relationship with her have changed as time has passed?

RETURN OF A PERPETRATOR

People who read novels and short stories know that it's not good if a character who has a significant role in the first part of a story just disappears. However, to Alex it's a surprise when Toril turns up at his office in London. What does she want?

In fiction, anger is the emotion of conflict, and conflict is critical to most drama. Even in the classics, the anger of fiction is usually a force of destruction. By contrast, in ordinary life, anger is usually quite different; most episodes occur with people we know and like or even love. The person to have shown this was James Averill. He asked people to keep diaries of incidents of anger. The diaries were structured like questionnaires. Participants were asked what happened in the incident, what was said, what was felt, and so on. Averill asked 80 married people and 80 unmarried students to look out for the next incident in which they were angry with someone, and to write details of it in the diary.

He also asked 80 people to fill out a diary form when they were the target of someone else's anger.

Averill found that people's purpose in anger was usually not to destroy, but to readjust a relationship in which something had gone wrong. About two-thirds of the participants who made a diary entry of feeling angry with someone else reported that incidents of anger occurred for them once or twice a week. The person with whom they were angry was usually someone such as a parent, a child, a spouse, a friend. Approximately two-thirds of angry people felt their anger had a negative quality. People who were the targets of other people's anger mostly felt even worse. However, despite this, 62 percent of angry people and 70 percent of those who were targets of other people's anger felt the angry incident was beneficial. Usually it functioned in long-term relationships to allow the participants to readjust something in that relationship.

For most people, an incident of anger starts with a sense of being wronged, or demeaned. Usually it ends by the people whom it concerns making some adjustment, coming to a reconciliation on a new basis. Averill proposed that anger has some of the quality of promising: the promise is to see the matter through until it is resolved, until the mutual status of the people involved has been readjusted. Another way of thinking about anger, and, indeed, about many other emotions, is as a kind of commitment to the other person involved.[5] In love, the commitment concerns cooperation, in anger it concerns conflict. For anger, when it is fully resolved, the commitment includes being different in the relationship.

In part V of "One Another," Alex is the target of David's anger. They are friends. They make it up, and re-commit to their relationship on a new basis. Alex will attend more closely to what he is doing, and give priority to it.

In part IV of the story, when Alex discovers that Toril must have led him on in order to steal the dissident's manuscript, he is angry. Furious. When, in part VI, she returns, she knows he will have been angry, but she wants to make it up with him. Now, he is in the position of power. He can make her suffer, and the first insult he inflicts is to keep her waiting for three hours. Then, he has sex with her. We may wonder why. On this occasion, the sex doesn't seem to occur because he wants to join with her. Is it perhaps because he wants to know what substance there may have been in his former feelings? Or—worse—does he want to assert his power over her?

Now rather than finding Toril transportingly desirable as he did in Helsinki, Alex sees her as pathetic. With the dissolution of the Soviet Union, she no longer has a job. She doesn't have many skills for the civilian world. She seems, indeed, to be trying to use her sexual skills to have Alex look after her. She doesn't know that such cloying dependency repels him.

Anger occurs when one's understanding of someone else and of how that other person should treat one is mistaken. When someone does something that is hurtful or demeaning, it damages an expectation that we thought was inherent in the relationship. We thought the person was thinking and feeling one thing, but the person's actions show he or she was thinking and feeling something else, and we become upset.

We can never know enough about other people. Fiction provides a safe place, in which we can explore, let our hearts go out to others, follow their plans, and make discoveries, but without the destruction that some of the discoveries would cause if they were to occur in our day-to-day lives.

When David was angry with Alex in part IV of "One Another," his anger was to renew the relationship. David is a generous person, with a continuing affection for Alex. The commitment of Alex's anger toward Toril seems very different. Although Alex knows that the Soviet system was his real opponent, and although he felt satisfaction in its collapse, a commitment to personal retribution remains. Just as Toril was not honest with him, he won't be honest with her. He rejects her, not face to face, but covertly.

If, in the story, we continue to identify with Alex, we might feel that Toril is paid out in her own coin. However, we may also start to feel for her. We know that she didn't behave well toward Alex, but perhaps we can imagine how an actress might have felt when her career was unsuccessful, imagine what her options might have been in a repressive country, and even imagine what she might have felt as someone who was patriotic to the USSR. Now, with the Soviet system dismantled and even discredited, she is left with few useful skills and not much of a sense of purpose. Is she to earn her living as a call girl?

What about Alex? He may still be angry when Toril returns—and we can understand this—but he conceals his motives. Should we re-evaluate how we feel about him?

One of the ways in which we might think about Alex's behavior is that he is not just angry with Toril in a way that enables him to be direct with her, but that he feels ashamed. Thomas Scheff and Suzanne Retzinger have argued that in Western society there is a taboo against shame. Not only is shame intensely painful—which is understandable—but we can't bear to admit to ourselves or anyone else when we feel ashamed.

It seems likely that Alex feels ashamed by what happened in Helsinki. David makes it clear that he thinks Alex should not have done what he did, and we readers know that in his liaison with Toril, Alex betrayed Sonya, whom he loved. Scheff and Retzinger argue that if shame occurs but is denied in oneself—suppressed or ignored—it does not just go away. It expresses itself in a more acceptable way, as anger. According to this proposal, much of male violence derives from the anger of suppressed shame and humiliation, from being abused in childhood, from being excluded at school, from being unable to fit in as an adolescent. In "One Another," instead of having things out with Toril in a way that might readjust their relationship, Alex is contemptous and cruel.

TOWARD AN ENDING

In chapter 5, I mentioned Aristotle's famous dictum that a story has a beginning, a middle, and an end. The end is usually a state of emotional resolution, such as the sadness of a tragic death or the happiness of a marriage. Sometimes there's a state of suspension, perhaps partly in the characters, but more importantly in the reader, a state of reflection perhaps or a state accompanied by curiosity about what might happen to the characters now that the events of the story have changed them.

In part VI of "One Another," Alex rejects Toril's second advance, and it's as if this brings to an end one strand of the story's plot: the story line about the attempt to smuggle the dissident's manuscript out of the Soviet Union and of Toril thwarting the attempt. The dissident's book is published and Alex has made something of his adventures in its foreword. Now, his antagonist, Toril, is subjected to a humiliating experience that compares with what Alex suffered at her hands.

In *The Sense of an Ending*, Frank Kermode argues that the idea of an ending—following a beginning and a middle—is one of the conventions of fiction that we find emotionally satisfying because it imposes order on time, which is, he says, disorderly. The sense of an ending, he proposes, is a form that gives consolation in a world that is formless, that consists of the incomprehensibility of being born, that subjects us to the ticks and tocks of time passing, and that involves contingencies such as illness and death. Though Kermode's book is engaging and thought provoking, I don't quite agree. Fiction and its emotions, I think, exist, not as a consolation for the inadequacies of our experience, not even to give them meaning, but to enable us to enlarge the meanings that we constantly develop in our lives.

One of these meanings is the theme of anger, with its arc of commitment toward a resolution. In life, this is usually to a reconciliation when things in a relationship have gone wrong. Fiction often emphasizes the unusual and almost always emphasizes the dramatic. That is why fictional anger so often ends in a destructive act. Perhaps the shock of this destructiveness may sometime enable us to step outside ourselves and see the usual in a new way, a deeper way. If, in fiction, after a beginning of hurt, and a middle of conflict, we come to an end of retribution, this pattern can be recognized because it is known in our experience, and in the script that it has formed.

Stories of anger in which the endpoint is total destruction of the antagonist are common, but, in this, fiction may veer too far from life. In "One Another," therefore, I have portrayed Alex's anger as more like that of everyday experience. He has been hurt. He is still angry, and the anger has an involuntary quality. He wants to inflict pain as we often do when we are angry. He is mean-minded as we often are when we are angry. The possibility of a readjustment of relationship with Toril is available. Alex could have told her how angry he has been, and that he didn't intend to start up with her again, not just because he wouldn't be able to get over his distrust of her, but because he has a commitment to another.

Alex foregoes this. Instead, he is willing to settle for an ending based on retribution, but this leaves something unresolved. We readers may feel it's not a proper conclusion. We move, therefore, toward the final part of the story of Alex and Sonya, within which the suspense story of smuggling and the amorous story of Alex and Toril have been embedded.

PART VII

When the Soviet Union broke up, changes occurred in Leningrad. Among them was the transformation of Sonya's mother's friendship with a certain Party official into a love affair. Her depression resolved.

Sonya made arrangements for her mother and her mother's companion to look after the apartment, and for herself to move to London. She enrolled for a PhD at the London School of Economics, to be supervised by a distinguished professor of political science. He'd come to respect her work during her master's degree. He arranged a research fellowship that was sufficient for her financial needs. The fellowship was prestigious. As well as independence, it gave Sonia confidence. Her work was recognized.

Sonya and Alex had been able to meet three times since they were in Warsaw. They had written frequently. They were enlivened at the prospect of being able, at last, to live together.

Alex converted the top floor of his house in Belsize Park, and made a study up there, with a desk and bookshelves, for Sonya. The space was lovely, with triangular ceiling shapes, up in the roof, and a window that caught the sun in the afternoon. He visited second-hand shops to look for an oak filing cabinet. He was pleased with one he found, which he placed next to the desk he'd bought for her at Heals. Another room on the top floor had an armchair, a couch, and a view. Up there, too, was a small bathroom that he'd renovated.

Alex went to meet Sonya at Heathrow, squeezed three large suitcases onto the back seat of his Mini Cooper, and brought her to his house.

They settled in well. Surprisingly quickly, too, Sonya was installed in her new department. She was delighted with her supervisor, and with the small office she shared with another PhD student. When the weather was fine she would walk down Haverstock Hill, over the canal at Camden Lock, past Euston Station. Sometimes she'd take a detour through Russell Square so that she could pass St George's Bloomsbury and the British Museum, and walk down Drury Lane. The buildings of Leningrad were interesting but, in her current mood, she found this London walk extraordinarily romantic.

.　.　.

Three weeks after Sonya had arrived, Alex came home to find her sitting in his kitchen. On the pinewood table in front of her was the dissident's book.

"I read your foreword," she said.

"Did you like it?"

"At the hotel in Helsinki, they had someone waiting for you."

"What do you mean?"

"You know what I mean."

Alex felt his heart beating. He heard himself lying.

"No."

"In your foreword you say that in a hotel in Helsinki you went to a bar, and that the manuscript was stolen from your room. You're not interested in bars. It doesn't take much to know who stole the manuscript. It was a woman."

Alex had been looking forward to seeing Sonya, to having dinner together. His stomach took a dreadful lurch, as if it were falling downward, dragging him with it. A hot flush flooded up his neck.

"The woman," said Sonya, quietly. "At the hotel or in the train?"

"In the train. In the compartment."

"The beauty of reserved seats."

Sonya closed her eyes, pursed her lips, and shook her head.

"Tall and blonde, with big tits and a Finnish passport," she said.

"Her passport was Swedish."

Whatever am I saying? he thought. Should I confess?

"You're not perceptive," she said. "I've seen you when you meet people who want something from you. They look at you with goo-goo eyes and listen to your every word and say things that you think are intelligent but which are designed to keep you talking so that you think that they think you're the most extraordinarily interesting person."

He closed his eyes. Everything was moving too fast. How had she worked this out? He'd been extremely careful in his foreword. Why had he written it at all?

"How is it that you don't know who to trust?" she said. "You could have trusted me."

Alex noticed Sonya's past tense.

"Why didn't you say you were going smuggling? I'd have told you what to look out for."

"How do you know?"

"How do I know! The people who do these things are very pleased with themselves. You should hear their contempt when they talk about a mark. They wouldn't raid the man's flat or arrest you when you picked the manuscript up. Much better to have it disappear in a foreign country. No fuss. I'm sure you haven't made a fuss."

"None at all."

"They arrange a woman. The manuscript disappears in Finland. She comes back with it. No more than the price of a train fare and a hotel room."

Alex had been standing as Sonya talked. Now he sat down at the table and reached out to hold her hands, which were clasped together, on the table. She withdrew them.

"I'm sorry," he said.

"I needn't ask whether you fucked her."

Alex looked at the table and shook his head faintly.

"You didn't or I needn't ask?"

"You needn't ask."

"Don't touch me," she said. "You're an asshole."

Suddenly she was in tears. She shook her head. "Go away," she shouted. "Just go away."

She sat and cried for several minutes. Alex wanted to comfort her.

"I never want to see you again." She was shouting again. "How could you?"

She stood up, ready to leave.

"You think in Leningrad, all those months and years, I haven't had offers. I'm friendly. I'm well connected. But what about you?"

"What about me?"

"Shut up."

Sonya walked across the kitchen, turned and walked back.

"I tried not to think about it," she said. She was no longer shouting. "The possibility. And here you are, jumping from one bed to another. You're an asshole."

"That's not it."

"You're totally self-involved. You don't think 'No, I'm with someone else.' You think 'Oh, how fascinating.'"

She walked to the door, fully composed now.

"That's it," she said.

"Don't go. I'm sorry. Tell me what I can do."

"I'll tell you what you can do. You're a wanker. You can go and buy one of those magazines the capitalist press so thoughtfully provides for people like you, blondes with big tits, and wank till you go blind."

. . .

That night Sonya slept upstairs on the couch that Alex had bought for her. Next day she went into her department. In the evening she announced that she was going to stay with one of her fellow PhD students who had a place in Lamb's Conduit Street. She took a suitcase. Although it was heavy, she didn't want Alex to carry it to the Tube for her.

He thought she wouldn't stick it out, but she did. The terrible row happened on a Monday. On Thursday, he wrote a note, and took it round to her department, to leave if she wasn't there. But she was there.

"Can we meet?" he said.

"I'll meet you tomorrow. Six o'clock, at the main entrance, in Houghton Street."

.   .   .

They went to a coffee shop. There wouldn't be shouting there. The place didn't do meals. It was due to close in an hour, and it wasn't crowded. They found a table in a corner.

"I thought that, after all this time, we'd be able to make it," she said.

"You've stopped calling me names."

"I'm doing a PhD that's important to me. You're doing what you enjoy, meeting people and publishing books. Russia is crazy now. We could have had a life together."

"We can have a life together. I'm very sorry. I totally screwed up."

"You didn't screw up, you went out screwing."

"I know. I know."

"I'm still angry. You're an asshole. D'you know that? Seeing you sitting there with a cup of coffee looking pathetic, I can't be bothered. I'm disappointed. You're a man, I suppose. No different from the rest."

Alex reached out across the table to try and take her hands. She let him take them.

"When you live with someone you make love. It's one of the things you do, like having dinner together and sleeping in the same bed. All those years, I've been trying to think: was it this or was it that that made our sex life delicate? Or was it some other thing, that you had or I had, or you did or I did, that made it not quite right between us in bed? Or was it just the way it was? Now I know."

"Now you know what?"

"If a tall blonde woman comes along you'd be off. She'd barely have to twitch."

"Please forgive me."

"It's not going to work between us."

"It was a lapse."

"How can I trust you? We had a commitment."

"I'm sorry."

"You're going to tell me it's been the only one."

Alex didn't reply.

"Whenever we made love, you'd have her in your mind, or someone like her. I'd know it wasn't me you were with."

Sonya was silent. She withdrew her hands from Alex's.

"I wouldn't be able to stop myself thinking of it," she said.

They sat silently for three or four minutes. Sonya knew that what she'd just said was cruel. She wondered whether it was true.

"It was very bad of me," said Alex. "We've got something important together. I know I've been bad. I can change. I'm in therapy. Please give me a chance."

"I've found a place in Bloomsbury," she said. "A room of my own, in a very good apartment with two other women."

Chapter 7

Other Minds

People who read a lot of fiction tend to have better understandings of others than people who read more nonfiction. This is because fiction is primarily about people's doings in the social world. Fiction offers a way of knowing more than we otherwise would about others and ourselves.

In part I of "One Another," Sonya said she and Alex had something between them that could not be broken. Now in part VII, although Sonya has moved to London to live with Alex, she rejects him and goes to live separately. Is it possible that Alex could make it up with her, start on a new footing after experiences that have affected him deeply, which may have changed him? Now that we readers know something of the minds of Alex and Sonya, what do we think will happen?

In chapter 5, I mentioned that, in poetry, the Petrarchan sonnet form contains a turning point between lines 8 and 9. In the Elizabethan sonnet form, in which William Shakespeare wrote, there is another turning point between lines 12 and 13. Some of the sonnets Shakespeare wrote had turning points in both places. I have used the pattern of two turning points in "One Another," so that in part VII of the story, after the first surprise of finding that Toril worked for the secret police, there is another surprise of Sonya's inferences after she's read Alex's preface to the dissident's book. The structure of the relationship between Alex and Sonya shifts.

In part I of "One Another," Sonya thought Alex loved her exclusively, but his actions in part III show that he felt differently. In real life, such revelations can be among the most painful of experiences. In fiction we can enjoy the revelations, we can enjoy feeling the anger and its urge toward retribution, perhaps because we can learn something about how people can behave unexpectedly, without the damage that such events would wreak in our day-to-day lives.

In part V of the story, Alex was the target of David's anger for failing to understand that he should have given priority to watching over the manuscript he was bringing back to London. In part VII, it's Sonya who is angry.

We may like to compare her anger with that of Alex toward Toril. Whereas he was deceptive, Sonya is straightforward. Whereas he was self-involved, she is engaged in the relationship. Whereas nothing was to be done in the relationship between Alex and Toril, in the relationship between Sonya and Alex, we may wonder about its future.

THEORY OF MIND

Sonya and Alex did not know each other's minds well enough. In developmental psychology, the topic of how we know other minds has come to be of great interest. Psychologists call it theory of mind, or perspective taking, or mind-reading. It's the idea that we each can develop implicit theories of what others may be thinking and feeling in the moment when we talk with them or, over the longer term, when we reflect on what kind of person they are and make a mental model of them. Psychologists call the longer-term understanding personality. In fiction it's called character.

Marcel Proust suggested that only in fiction can we really come to know others, and that from this knowledge we can become better able to know others in our ordinary life. In *Le Temps Retrouvé* the last book of his long novel, *À la Recherche du Temps Perdu*, he wrote:

> Only through literary art can we escape from our selves and know the perspective of another on the world, which is not the same as our own, and which contains views of landscapes that would otherwise have remained as unknown as any there may be on the moon (257–258, my translation).

Jane Austen's *Pride and Prejudice* is about Elizabeth Bennet coming to know the mind of Mr. Darcy. She comes to form, as it were, a theory or mental model of who he is. The novel is also about Darcy who, to start with, is disdainful of Elizabeth. As the story continues, he comes to form a theory of her mind. And—unlike many romance stories in which people fall in love at a mere glance—it's only by coming to know each other that Elizabeth and Darcy come to love each other.

In "One Another," although Alex and Sonya are close, neither has a very good theory of the other's mind in the first part of the story so that, in part VII, the realization of what the other has been thinking and feeling comes as a shock to both and, if I have written the story properly, it may bring a (smaller) shock to you, the readers.

In literary theory, the movement to see much of the subject matter of fiction in terms of theory of mind has been energized recently by Lisa Zunshine. She argues that certain kinds of fiction, such as detective stories, are about coming to know others even when they are trying to conceal what they are thinking and feeling. Such problems of theory of mind, says Zunshine, are the typical subject matter of novels and short stories, even those that don't seem to be detective stories.

In most fiction, there are questions of what characters are really up to. We enjoy those questions, says Zunshine, because they give us problems of theory of mind. Theory of mind is what we humans are good at, she continues, and because we enjoy what we are good at, our thinking through of theory-of-mind problems is the reason we enjoy fiction.

In children, theory of mind starts at about the age of four. This conclusion became firmly established in psychology with the publication of an ingenious experiment by Heinz Wimmer and Josef Perner. They told children a story in which a little boy, Maxi, had some chocolate that he put in a blue cupboard. He went out to play and, while he was out, his mother used some of the chocolate for a cake. Then she put the rest of the chocolate in a different place, in a green cupboard. The children in the experiment were asked: "When Maxi comes back indoors, he would like some of his chocolate. Where will he look for it?" Children under about four typically said: "In the green cupboard." That's where the chocolate was. That's what they knew, and so that's where they thought Maxi would look. However, children aged four and over tended to say, "In the blue cupboard." They knew that this was where Maxi had left his chocolate, and they knew, too, that because Maxi did not know that his mother had put it in a different place, this is where he would look. By age four, children understand that other people can know things that are different from what they themselves know. The same applies to children's own selves: Alison Gopnik and Janet Astington found that only after the age of about four do children begin to know that what they think and feel now can be different from what they thought and felt in the past.

In chapter 1, I said that character is all-important in fiction. It's all-important, too, in everyday life, both the understanding of other people and the understanding of ourselves. We humans live by cooperation. How could we cooperate without knowing others and without being able to rely on them? Part of the enjoyment of fiction, I think, is not just the hedonistic pleasure of suspense and being taken out of ourselves, but the deeper enjoyment of being able to understand more about others and ourselves. It is based on being able to improve our understanding of other minds. Just as when a love relationship starts, one delights in coming to know the loved one because one wants one's love to extend to everything that person is, in fiction, we want to understand protagonists and other characters.

Of all the components that authors deliberately place into their works of fiction, character remains, perhaps, the most important. If, as a reader, you are not engaged with at least one character of a story, you tend not to read on. The psychological origin is deep, and the reason has recently started to become clearer. It used to be thought that the reason we humans have very large brains as compared with other animals was because we are very clever, because we make tools, because in our evolution we were cunning at hunting. But the likely reason is that we need big brains because we are very social—more social than other vertebrates.

Robin Dunbar has proposed that we need large brains because we know a large number of people in our social world, up to about 150, in sufficient detail that we can describe something of the character of each of them. We make mental models of them, for instance: "Fred is affectionate, but I do wish he wouldn't grumble all the time." And so on. The maximum size of the social group in which chimpanzees live is 50, that is to say 50 individuals whom each member of the group knows as friends, relatives, allies, enemies. Chimpanzees are our closest relatives. The fossil record and DNA studies show that the line that led to them split off from the line that led to us about six million years ago. Our brains became larger because, as Dunbar explains, our ancestors lived in social groups that became progressively larger. The size of 150 is about that to which villages grow before, when space is available, they split into two. It's about the number of people in urban societies whom people know well enough to have had a meal with them, to ask a favor of them, to be interested in what their children and other relatives are doing.

The human brain is exceptionally large because it has to house mental models for three times as many individuals as can be held by the brain of a chimpanzee, and our models have more detail. The people we know well, we know sufficiently not just to sketch the person's character, and not just to recall interactions we have had with them. Our models include ideas about their interactions with others in our social group. About 70 percent of human conversations are about the plans and doings of ourselves and people we know. We are able to talk and exchange anecdotes and gossip about others, that is to say exchange bits of information to improve our mental models of each other: "Betty is still loyal, even though she was terribly badly treated." It is likely that our enjoyment of conversing about ourselves and others is the origin of our interest in stories.

In an experiment devised by Raymond Mar, members of the research group in which I work have found that, the more fiction people read, the better is their understanding of other people, that is to say, the better their theory of mind. We measured the amount of fiction and nonfiction that participants had read, and then gave them two tests of social ability. One was a test of adult theory of mind and empathy. It's called the Mind in the Eyes test. In it, participants are shown a set of photographs of people's eyes, as if seen through a letter box, so that the rest of their faces cannot be seen. For each picture, participants have to say what they think the person was feeling. For one photograph, the options are "joking, flustered, desire, convinced." The second test of social ability was of interpersonal perception. Participants watched video clips of ordinary people in interaction. For each clip, they had to answer a question about what was going on in the interaction.

We found that the more fiction people read, the better they were at the Mind in the Eyes test. They had better theory of mind and empathy. By comparison, if people read predominantly non-fiction, they tended to do worse at the Mind in the Eyes test. Fiction readers were also somewhat better at the test of interpersonal perception. We repeated the experiment with a larger sample, using only the Mind in the Eyes test as outcome. In this experiment we excluded the possibility that the result could have due to people with the personality trait of high interest in others being drawn to fiction. We measured readers' personality traits and a number of other individual differences. We looked to see how closely each individual characteristic was associated with reading habits, and then controlled for it (that is to say, we subtracted it out). When we had controlled for all these characteristics of the individual, we still found that those who read more fiction had better theory of mind and empathy. That is to say, people who read more fiction had better theory of mind, independently of what kinds of personality they had: it looks as if reading more fiction improved people's theory of mind.[1]

In a study on children, Raymond Mar, with Jennifer Tackett and Chris Moore, found that children who had more exposure to story books and movies had better theory of mind than those who had less exposure. Theory of mind, in the experiment with children, was measured by five tasks. The way in which exposure to story books and movies predicted children's theory of mind was robust, even when effects of their vocabulary, the level of their parents' education, and other such variables had been controlled for (subtracted out). Children's exposure to television, however, did not predict their abilities at theory of mind. In another follow-up, Mar did an experiment in which he randomly assigned people to read either a fiction story or a nonfiction piece from the *New Yorker*. Immediately after reading, those who read the piece of fiction did better on a test of social reasoning than those who read the piece of nonfiction. Reading fiction put them into a state of preparedness to reason about the social world.

With theory of mind, we not only make mental models of others but also mental models of others' mental models. In fact, we humans can maintain several layers of models of what others are believing, wanting, feeling, and so on. Dunbar has enumerated the layers of such mental states required for certain kinds of literature. Thus, he writes (p. 162), in *Othello*, Shakespeare

> *intended* [1] that his audience *realize* [2] that the eponymous moor *believed* [3] that his servant Iago was being honest when he claimed to *know* [4] that his beloved Desdemona *loved* [5] Cassio.

In "One Another," I, the writer, *intended* (1) that you, the reader, *realize* (2) that Sonya *suspects* (3) that Alex was *misled* (4) by a woman who inveigled Alex into bed because she *wanted* (5) to steal the manuscript.

This kind of embedding occurs, not just among characters in a work of fiction, but also between the writer and the reader. In his book on the novel, Orhan Pamuk (p. 153) has written:

At every detail, the writer thinks that the reader will think that this detail was experienced. And the reader thinks that the writer wrote with the thought that the reader will think it has been experienced. The writer, in turn, thinks that he wrote that detail thinking that the reader will have thought of this, too. This play of mirrors is valid for the writer's imagination as well.

Research over the last 30 years has shown that our minds are much more concerned with social life than had previously been thought. A great deal of our mental machinery is geared to working out what others think, and what they think we think, and so on.

When we human beings play, we do so socially. In childhood there are hide-and-seek and chase games, progressing to ball games. By adulthood this motivation can move to watching sports on television. Fiction is a form of play about the social world.[2] Rather than chasing around a playground, we read books about people being pursued in detective stories. Rather than playing with dress-up clothes and toys, we imagine ourselves as other people in places we would never visit.

The real reason, the deep reason, why fiction is all about the emotions is that it's about the social world that we live in, of selves and others, to which our brains and minds are attuned. Emotions are both signs of what we value, and signals that things might not be as we had thought. We are built to operate in, and enjoy, the social world. We enjoy meeting a new person who becomes a friend. We want to find out about that person, to know her or his mind. We start to take an interest in the person's projects, become happy when these succeed, become distressed when the person is thwarted by someone else.

So fiction isn't just something that's been made up. It's about worlds of the imagination in which those matters in which we are most interested in our day-to-day lives are depicted, so that we experience the emotions, but without some of the devastating effects that events could have in our lives. It's a form of play. Just as we can enjoy the competition of chess—combat between two imaginary medieval armies—without the danger of being killed, so we can enjoy entering into a role, such as the role of Alex, without being hit in the back by a border guard's rifle butt. We can enjoy an encounter with an exotic new lover without betraying a person we love.

CHARACTERS AS FRIENDS

The literary theorist Wayne Booth proposed that the best way to think of a fictional character, or narrator, or even author, is as a friend. Although the relationship with a character doesn't have the comings and goings of friendship in ordinary life, psychologists have found that it has some of the same properties.

Wendi Gardner and Megan Knowles found that people feel close to favorite fictional characters in ways that are like being close to a friend. In their paper on these issues, they start with a quotation from the 1922 children's story, *The Velveteen Rabbit*, by Margery Williams, in which a boy is given a stuffed velveteen rabbit for Christmas. The rabbit is mocked by the boy's other, more expensive, mechanical toys who think they are real, but the skin horse explains that being Real isn't about how you are made. You become Real when you are really loved. The velveteen rabbit becomes the boy's constant companion until the boy falls ill with scarlet fever. The rabbit has become shabby, and is to be burned with bedclothes and other potentially infectious things.

The velveteen rabbit sheds a real tear, and magically he is transformed into a real rabbit. Next spring, when the boy has recovered, he sees two rabbits hopping about in the woods behind his house and thinks the markings on one of them seem familiar. The book's last sentence is: "But he never knew that it really was his own Bunny, come back to look at the child who had first helped him to be Real."

Like this rabbit, fictional characters become real when they are loved or liked, or, at least, when we take a strong interest in them. In their paper, Gardner and Knowles report a survey in which they found that better-liked favorite television characters were perceived as more real than equally familiar but less-liked characters in the same series. With a further set of participants, they then did an experiment: a variation of a well established procedure in which it has been found that people do tasks differently when they are in the presence of a friend than when they are with someone they don't know. Gardner and Knowles found similar effects. People who saw a picture of their favorite television character did tasks in the way they would in the presence of a friend, whereas those who saw a picture of a familiar but less-liked television character did the tasks as they would in the presence of a stranger.

Jaye Derrick and colleagues continued this line of research and found that people became less lonely when they watched favorite television programs that had their favorite characters in them. In watching these programs, people felt a sense of belonging, and the programs buffered them against deteriorations of mood, and from a sense of rejection that they might fear from real friends. Fictional characters aren't, of course, as important as real friends, but they can become more important than mere acquaintances.

For a fictional character to come alive so that the reader feels warmly toward him or her, like a character in a television series of the kind Gardner and Knowles studied, the relationship must have time to grow—for instance, over many episodes—so the character is seen in many contexts. This, of course, has been achieved in detective fiction by such characters as Arthur Conan Doyle's Sherlock Holmes and Agatha Christie's Miss Marple, both of whom appear in many stories.

I suspect we all have favorite fictional characters, and Hollywood has traded on this idea in creating stars who are likable, even lovable, so that we like to see them over and over again, and even want to be like them. Cary Grant is quoted as saying, "Everybody wants to be Cary Grant…Even I want to be Cary Grant," but, of course, he wasn't Cary Grant. He was the actor who played that figure. In fact, film stars—not just the characters they play—are fictional, in that they have to act not only the parts they play in movies but to act the part of celebrity. If you knew them in ordinary life they would be different from the images their promoters offer us, that journalists write about, and that are seen in television interviews. That, in part, I think is why it becomes a juicy item of news when a hunk known for romantic roles with women comes out as gay, or when it turns out that a woman who plays a vamp is painfully shy. I still retain an image of Julie Christie, one of the most appealing film actresses of my generation, whom I remember seeing in John Schlesinger's film *Billy Liar* as she walked along a city street swinging her handbag. It was a pleasure, but also a shock, to meet her at a political protest in London. Wearing her anorak and walking shoes, and without movie makeup, she didn't seem so much different from all the rest of us.

For a character to come alive, the reader needs to become emotionally attracted to him or her, and this occurs because the character is likable, or is unusual, or is in a situation that is interesting.

The writer offers suggestions, but only the reader or audience member can bring the character to life, make that character real. Without the reader or watcher, a story is a set of marks on a page or a shimmer of lights on a screen. For a plot to work, we tend to become anxious on a character's behalf when his or her project runs into trouble. We turn the pages to see what will happen. We hope to reach some relief and understanding in finding how the character negotiates setbacks and accomplishes some version of what he or she sets out to do, even though it may not be in the way that the character or we expected.

CHARACTERS AS IDEAL TYPES

Do we actually become like characters we read about or watch? Fear of this is one of the reasons people who favor censorship want to control the kinds of fictional characters we're exposed to. They cite the power of personal example, and worry that if we encounter fictional characters who are dishonest, addicted, violent, or lewd, we may ourselves become dishonest, addicted, violent, or lewd. Drawing on such concerns, there has been a large amount of research on whether media violence encourages violence in the behavior of young people. Recent evidence indicates that there are effects of this kind,[3] although some conclusions remain controversial.

What about effects in the other direction? Jonathan Haidt has presented research in which he shows that, when in a story, one reads or sees someone doing something generous or altruistic, the emotional experience of the reader or viewer is heightened and happy. He calls the effect elevation. Alice Isen has conducted a long series of studies, which show that when people are made happy by being told they did very well in a task, or even by being given a small gift, they are more likely to behave altruistically to others. In "One Another," David is generous to Alex, in renewing his friendship and being considerate after he was angry. In readers, this might give rise to a small moment of elevation. Some stories and films are all about moments of generosity. I think the reason many people think *Casablanca* is a moving film is, not only that its stars—Humphrey Bogart and Ingrid Bergman—are extraordinarily appealing, but also that, at the end of the film, the Bogart character acts with great generosity. It seems possible both in the world of the film, and in the world in which we live, and we feel elevated by this.

A group of researchers led by John Johnson asked 519 scholars and students of nineteenth-century British literature to assess the personality of 435 characters in 143 canonical Victorian novels. The scholars and students were asked to rate characters' goals, their success in achieving these goals, their preferences and strategies for attaining a mate, as well as their personality traits. There was good agreement among the raters about what each of the characters was like. For instance, one of the best-depicted characters in British fiction, Dorothea Brooke in George Eliot's *Middlemarch*, was rated as low in dominance, very high in constructive effort, about average in romance, and moderately high in nurturing tendencies. The researchers found that the associations between traits of the literary characters agreed well with the comparable associations found in research on the personalities of actual people, and this indicates that the canonical Victorian novelists were good intuitive psychologists, and accurate in their perceptions of others. One interesting difference emerged, however. The characters in canonical novels were higher than the average of modern populations in the tendency to value social harmony between self and others, and among people in the social group.[4] This may have the effect of encouraging readers of these novels toward greater empathy and cooperation with others.

A study by Marisa Bortolussi and her colleagues illuminates the question of what enables us to identify with literary characters.[5] Bortolussi's research team selected four passages, each of about 1,000 words, from contemporary novels, two with male protagonists and two with female protagonists. For each passage with a male protagonist, they wrote a version of the same passage with a female protagonist, and for each passage with a female protagonist, they wrote a version with a male protagonist. They prepared versions in English (for Canadian readers) and in German (for German readers). Previous research[6] has tended to find that males tended to prefer male protagonists and females to prefer female protagonists. With their clever manipulation of assigning people to the same stories but with different-sexed protagonists, Bortolussi and her colleagues found both male and female readers—in Canada and Germany—preferred and identified better with male protagonists. Both males and female readers agreed more strongly with an item that stated, "I feel I can understand and appreciate the main character and situation of the story," and one that stated, "I would like to continue reading to find out what happens next in the story," when the protagonist was male as compared with being female.

The researchers explain this effect in terms of the actor-observer bias (which I discussed in chapter 1). In general, say Bortolussi and her colleagues, men in Western societies tend to be seen as acting in response to circumstances ("he did what he had to"), whereas women tend more often to be seen in terms of their personality ("she behaved emotionally").

Both men and women are drawn to characters who are portrayed as like us, in the sense that we experience ourselves as acting in response to circumstances. In Western society, our social stereotypes are that men come closer to this ideal than women. This is enough to make it easier in stories to understand and to identify with a male protagonist, the kind of character who acts in response to the situation he is in, than with a female protagonist, the kind of character who acts because of her personality.

HOW WELL CAN WE KNOW FICTIONAL CHARACTERS?

Sometimes we can know fictional characters better than people in our day-to-day lives. But, of course, we don't get to know all characters equally; those we come to know well have the largest emotional effects on us.

In *Aspects of the Novel*, E.M. Forster makes a distinction that has become famous between fictional characters who are round and those who are flat. A flat character in fiction—more or less a cardboard cutout—represents a single characteristic that can be expressed in a single sentence. Forster's example is of Charles Dickens's Mrs. Micawber. "I won't desert Mr Micawber," she says, and she doesn't. Flat characters exhibit a single desire, and hence give rise to a mental model with just one component. Their role is to fulfill a function in the plot of a story. By contrast, round characters seem to come alive in their own right, beyond the story, alive in the mind in the way a friend does. Forster achieved several round characters in his novels, including Mrs. Moore and Dr. Aziz in *A Passage to India.* Among my favorite round characters are Dorothea Brooke in George Eliot's *Middlemarch*, and Pierre in Leo Tolstoy's *War and Peace.* Something the size of a novel seems to be needed to enable a character to become fully round, just as it's necessary to know someone for a long time, to see them with other people of different kinds and in many situations, and to love them, before one really comes to know them so that they come roundly alive in one's mind.

I'd like Alex and Sonya to become round in my story, so that you as a reader can feel strongly in relation to them. However, apart from whether I have the skill to enable this, I doubt whether the short story is a form that can enable full roundness to be accomplished. Not only is it too short, but also the function of a short story is rather different, as Frank O'Connor has shown in the *The Lonely Voice*. A novel tends to be about the unfolding of a life of a character in relation to society. In such circumstances, a character can become round, and someone with whom we identify strongly can emerge. By contrast, a short story is a glimpse, a turning point in a life. And typically, as O'Connor poignantly shows, a protagonist in a short story is often on the edge of society, often lonely. One may identify with such a one, but more often we tend to regard the events that affect him or her with consternation, sometimes from a bit of a distance, perhaps more with a sense of sympathy than with full empathy. Necessarily, a short story has just a few episodes. The form is pared down to enable us to get just a few clear glimpses of these episodes.[7]

In a short story, I think, one can achieve for one's characters, not roundness, but something in between roundness and flatness: three or four glimpses, so that the character is seen from more than one viewpoint, as one might meet someone interesting just a few times. I think the same is achieved in the better kind of detective fiction, in which characters are not seen deeply in the way that can occur in the great novels of the nineteenth century but as studies of just one aspect of who they are—an aspect, usually, of how they are driven by a desire that makes them susceptible to temptation. This is still enough for us to become interested in them.

As Anne Bartsch and her colleagues have shown, people become very experienced with the genres of novels they like to read and movies they like to watch. Entertainment is everywhere. It's one of the most pervasive features of modern life. Much research has been done on how people choose the entertainment they read and see. Researchers tend to call the principle that supports such choosing "mood-management." People come to know what kinds of emotions they enjoy in fiction, and they choose what to read or see to help manage their mood. For instance, someone whose job involves a lot of responsibility and anxiety may choose a certain kind of detective story to read at the end of the day. Within it he or she can enter a world that produces anxiety but of a kind that—unlike the reader's day-to-day anxiety—will be satisfactorily resolved. A man whose life is humdrum may like to enter a world in which a protagonist bravely overcomes seemingly insuperable obstacles and becomes a hero. A woman who feels lonely may choose romantic novels and films in which she can fall in love with men who are altogether more suitable than those she usually meets. What one hopes for in fiction, I think, includes a resonance with a theme, a *rasa* (of a heroic, a romantic, or some other kind), some curiosity about how the plot will turn out, and some engagement with the issue of character.

Here, in chapter 7, I've come in a circle back to the issues of character with which I started in chapter 1. We return in this way, perhaps to see more deeply why, at the center of our enjoyment of fiction, there is an enjoyment of character. At this center is the possibility of engaging with characters who are both like and unlike ourselves, the possibility of acting in ways that we can recognize but would not necessarily do in our day-to-day lives, the possibility of feeling a flush of emotion which, in our ordinary lives we might prefer to have avoided.

Chapter 8

Reflection

Fiction can be thought of as a set of simulations of selves in the social world. These simulations can be exchanged with the simulations of consciousness, in a way that enables us to reflect on them

In this final chapter, I'd like to consider with you the question of what a piece of fiction is. I'll draw on some of the themes of my recent book, *Such Stuff as Dreams: The Psychology of Fiction*, and reflect on how they affect our understandings of emotions in fiction, including our overall experience of the story "One Another."

A story is not so much a flow of actions and events—this happened and then that—as a flow of emotions and thoughts in the mind of the reader. The emotions of a story can be just emotions, as in the prototypical thriller: something bad happens to the protagonist, we feel angry on his or her behalf, and take part with the protagonist in a pursuit of the perpetrator until vengeance is wreaked. More subtle stories enable the emotions and thoughts that the story prompts in the reader—which the reader would not otherwise have had—to suggest reflections on new understandings of others and the self, or on old understandings seen in new ways.

SIMULATION

In my view, the way fiction works in the mind and brain is that when we read, hear, or watch a story, we create and run a simulation of selves in the social world.[1] This kind of simulation was invented long before computers. It could not run on a computer. It can only run on a mind constructed to understand itself and others.

The principal idea in the founding book on the psychology of fiction, Aristotle's *Poetics*, is *mimesis*. Stephen Halliwell has shown that the term has two families of meanings. One family is of representation, imitation, or copying, and these terms are the usual translations of *mimesis* in English. The other, less recognized but arguably more important, family of meanings is of world making, or simulation. In his *Poetics*, it was this second meaning on which Aristotle concentrated.

> A poetic *mimesis*, then ought to be unified... since the plot is
> [a] *mimesis* of an action, the latter ought to be both unified
> and complete, and component events ought to be so firmly
> compacted that if any one of them is shifted to another place,
> or removed, the whole is loosened up and dislocated; for an
> element whose addition or subtraction makes no perceptible
> extra difference is not really a part of the whole (p. 32).

Aristotle certainly considered imitative aspects of fiction, and they are important. A fictional world needs some imitative correspondence with the ordinary world. Identification with a character in fiction can be thought of as a kind of inner imitation, but fiction works principally not because elements in a play, movie, or printed story simply imitate their equivalents in ordinary life. The language of epics and dramas that Aristotle discussed were very different from everyday speech. These stories were written in specially heightened poetic language. What Aristotle is mainly concerned with in *Poetics* are overall structures, how episodes fit together to make a meaningful whole, a created world that offers insights we could not easily attain in other ways. The ideas of coherence that he stresses are ideas of *mimesis* as world building, meaning simulation in the service of emotionally perfused understanding.

In *Poetics*, Aristotle's proposal about emotions is that, in a tragic drama, the playgoer experiences pity and fear, and that these emotions undergo *katharsis*. Like *mimesis*, this term has been sedulously mistranslated. In English, the usual translations are purification or purgation. Thus, one translation occurs as follows.

> Tragedy, then, is a process of imitation [*mimesis*] of an action which has serious implications...enacted by the persons themselves and not presented through narrative; through a course of pity and fear completing the purification [*katharsis*] of tragic acts which have those emotional characteristics (Translation by Else, p. 25).

Here is a different translation of the last part of this passage.

> ...presented in the form of action, not narration; by means of pity and fear bringing about the purgation [*katharsis*] of such emotions (Translation by Dorsch, p. 39).

The idea in both these translations is that there is something wrong with emotions in tragic acts or with the emotions generally so that they must be purified or purged. It is as if emotions must be either turned into something more spiritual or gotten rid of inside the theater so that, when one goes back into the ordinary world after the play, they will no longer interfere with our lives.

The word *katharsis* occurs only once in *Poetics*, and this has given rise to the idea that it is unusual and mysterious. Martha Nussbaum has shown that this is not so. The term was common, says Nussbaum. It and related words (*kathairo*, *katharos*) were used frequently by Plato and Aristotle. The term meant clearing up, clarification, clearing away obstacles, including the cognitive meaning of seeing clearly without obscuration, or seeing without obstacles to understanding. Nussbaum explains that the meanings of purification and purgation that have entered English translations come from derived ideas: the first a spiritual meaning, to transform in order to be without obscuring blemish, and the second a medical one, to clear an obstructed gut. Such derived meanings in this passage in *Poetics* are implausible and unhelpful. The line of Aristotle's thinking makes it far more likely that he had in mind a straightforwardly cognitive meaning of clearing away obstacles to understanding. Nussbaum's translation of the lines for which I offered two translations, above, is:

> The function of tragedy is to accomplish through pity and fear, a clarification (or illumination) concerning experiences of the pitiable and fearful kind (p. 391).[2]

Overall, Aristotle argues that epics and plays deepen our understanding of lives, of actions, and of the implications of these actions, which occur "according to probability or necessity."

The modern meaning of simulation is only about 60 years old. It came into use with the introduction of computers. However, as the preceding discussion of Aristotle shows, the idea is older.

Alongside the idea of *mimesis*-as-imitation, the parallel idea of *mimesis*-as-simulation has been central for some literary artists and for some of those who wrote thoughtfully about art. For instance, William Shakespeare made this idea central to his art, and called it "dream" as in *A Midsummer Night's Dream*, and (from *The Tempest*) "We are such stuff as dreams are made on."

According to this theory, a piece of fiction offers the reader the materials to compose a simulation of selves in the social world, a kind of dream, in which some matters can be understood more clearly than in day-to-day life. The structure of the story-dream is that selves as protagonists, and other characters, have intentions and that as intentions unfold into actions they meet vicissitudes. One may enter such structures and experience one's emotions in a set of circumstances far more varied than those we would encounter in our ordinary life.

The cold-war antagonism between the Soviet Union and the West exists no more, but issues of antagonism remain, and so, in the dream world that I've invited you to create in "One Another," we can explore them.

CONSCIOUSNESS

In philosophy, the traditional view of consciousness accords with introspection. We decide consciously what to do, then do it. However, recent evidence suggests this is misleading. One line of evidence derives from the work of Benjamin Libet, and shows that at least some actions are initiated before conscious decisions to act can occur. Another line, from Richard Nisbett and Timothy Wilson, is that, when subjected to unobtrusive social maneuvers, people can be induced to act in certain ways, but they can remain unconscious of why they acted as they did.

In response to evidence of this kind, Roy Baumeister and E. J. Masicampo have proposed that the function of consciousness is not the immediate initiation of actions.[3] Instead, it is to create simulations of ourselves. These simulations interrelate memory, current understandings of the self in the social world, and evaluation of future actions. Conscious thought enables us to explain ourselves verbally to ourselves and others, and also to compose our minds. Here's what Baumeister and Masicampo say:

> The influence of conscious thought on behavior can be vitally helpful but is mostly indirect. Conscious simulation processes are useful for understanding the perspectives of social interaction partners, for exploring options in complex decisions, for replaying past events (both literally and counterfactually) so as to learn, and for facilitating participation in culture in other ways (p. 945).

As Michael Tomasello has shown, to become, in the course of development, a fully functioning human is to understand ourselves as agents and to understand others also as agents. Such understandings are central to all the languages of the world. Consciousness arises from these developments and, by adolescence, it includes verbal abilities of being able to think of ourselves in narrative terms, of being able to visualize images, and of being able to relate autobiographical memories to future possibilities of action. By means of conscious thought, we become able to construct mental models that we can consult and modify. These models, or simulations, can include language-based ideas and visual images that can themselves become objects of thought in problem solving, thinking about our friends and relations, and projecting ourselves into the future.[4]

For a long time, fiction has been seen as augmenting the functions of consciousness. Baumeister and Masicampo give us a good way of thinking about how this might occur. Fiction consists of crafted and externalized simulations, twins of our internal simulations. Plays, novels, short stories, and films can then be internalized by us, assimilated, to add to the construction of our simulations in our theater of inner consciousness.

Baumeister and Masicampo give an example of a use of consciousness in a piece of planning:

> ...when one has a plane to catch tomorrow, one typically engages in a simulation that calculates backward from the plane's takeoff time, allowing for airport procedures, the trip to the airport, and perhaps the hotel checkout before that, so one knows at what time to commence the sequence of acts. All the information used for this simulation is already in the mind, so conducting the simulation does not bring in new information from the environment...These simulations work remarkably well in enabling people to be on time for their flights without having to spend many extra hours at the airport (p. 955).

I call the means by which this kind of function is accomplished the planning processor, the device by which we arrange our projects in the world. It requires a mental model of how the physical and social world works, and it enables us to arrange possible actions into a plan within this world. This device then also affords an understanding of how, as a reader, one creates a literary simulation. The writer gives the reader cues and suggestions to simulate—create a mental model of—an imagined world. Empathetic identification with a character occurs when, in response to the writer's invitation, the reader puts aside her or his own goals and concerns, inserts the goals and plans of the character into his or her own planning processor, and mentally enacts the plot. The emotions that then occur are empathetic emotions in relation to the plot's plans, actions, and outcomes, not the character's but the reader's own.

Baumeister and Masicampo's idea of the simulations of consciousness is very similar to the idea of the simulations of fiction that I proposed in *Such Stuff as Dreams*. How encouraging that the simulations of consciousness and the simulations of fiction seem so readily interchangeable.

When tracking the actions of a fictional character, a reader or audience member uses this planning ability within his or her mental simulation. In fiction, an author gives the reader information about the setting and about the protagonist's goals and then starts readers off on a plan of the protagonist. Next, the author indicates what events occur in relation to the protagonist's action, including those in the minds of the protagonist and other characters. As we put aside our own goals and plans and take on those of a protagonist, we enter that character's patterns of conscious thought and the story enables us to know outcomes of actions.

According to Jaak Panksepp, emotion was the original form of consciousness during evolution. It's been important in its energization of plans and in its reworkings of plans that have not gone as expected. Also, as language became part of human life, emotion has been one of conversation's principal topics.

Conversation can be thought of as externalization and exchange of pieces of consciousness with particular people to whom we relate. Emotions are arbiters of our values (evaluations of events in relation to our concerns), the means of aligning ourselves with others, of calibrating ourselves with them in our social world, and of configuring our relationships with others.

These reasons all contribute to why emotions should be so central to consciousness.

Conversation and anecdote were the original ways of enabling us to import pieces of simulation from someone else into our own conscious simulations. Crafted stories of oral recitation and enacted drama then entered human cultural experience. Written stories came later, and movies later still, but all these narrative forms have similar properties, of being narrative simulations that we can incorporate into our own consciousness.

MEMORY

As I discussed in chapter 1, one of the ways in which we experience emotions in stories is by emotional memories entering the reader's simulation either in the form of a reliving of some autobiographical incident or in the form of emotions based on universals (*rasas*) that are part of remembered experience. Near the beginning of chapter 3 of his book, *Literary Reading*, Michael Burke gives a quotation from *The Ebb Tide*, by Robert Louis Stevenson (based on a draft by his stepson, Lloyd Osbourne) about an Englishman who has disgraced himself in a lifetime of failure. He is on the island of Tahiti, "on the beach," meaning washed up. His only possession is a copy of Virgil's *Aeneid*, into which he dips from time to time. Prompted by its pages there arise in his mind not images from the *Aeneid's* setting of the Roman World of 2000 years ago, but memories of the England of his childhood when he had to study the *Aeneid*: "the busy school room, the green playing fields, holidays at home, and the perennial roar of London" (Stevenson, p. 174). This is a striking image, which suggests that memories evoked by a story can be very individual indeed.

Part of the task for a writer is to offer a story to readers in a way that enables them to experience parts of it as resonances with memories of their own lives. In doing so, they can relate a memory to their current self, but in a new setting. Perhaps, then, they are able to reflect on it, feel its emotion, and experience some change in themselves. It's something of this kind that Burke suggests in a model of reading that he calls "oceanic." It's like making oneself part of a wave. To begin with, as we prepare to read, we must be in the right mood, get into the right kind of place—maybe a bed or armchair—and arrange ourselves in the right posture. As our own resources of mood and memory start up they mingle, like the waters of a gathering wave, with the book we start to read and, as the story progresses, the wave rises with a gathering tension until at last it breaks and the tension is released. With this release, the reader may experience what James Joyce has called an epiphany.[5] In this, however, the principal purpose of fiction is not yet fully achieved. The full purpose, as Scott Fitzgerald wrote to Ernest Hemingway, includes an "appeal to the lingering after-effects in the reader's mind."[6] Burke concludes that "reading does not begin or end when eyes apprehend the words on the page" (p. 255).

Reading a story about a protagonist with whom we share some characteristics is likely to trigger more emotional memories than reading about someone very different from ourselves. In "One Another," I have written about a train journey. I hope that my depiction might evoke for you memories of train journeys you have taken, and at the same time, enable you to use your experience of such journeys to bring the scene alive. Such memories show what Burke means when he says that reading a piece of fiction begins before the eyes start to traverse the words on the page. The fact that we can discuss a story after reading it means that Burke is right, too, that the effects of reading can linger.

Following the usual translation of Aristotle's term *mimesis*, many people have thought that the function of art is to imitate life. However, if what I'm saying here about stories as simulations is correct, then, perhaps, the more important movement is for life to imitate art. We ourselves, in our own lives, can change the simulation, which is our consciousness, and thereby change ourselves by choosing carefully the fictional simulations with which we engage, and by taking them in.

THE DRAMATURGICAL PERSPECTIVE

In *As You Like It*, Shakespeare wrote "All the world's a stage." This is usually taken as a metaphor, but Erving Goffman took it literally, and set about investigating how it could be. He concluded that yes, indeed, we do give dramatic performances: presentations of our selves in everyday life. As such, there can be an ambiguity that enables, in fiction and in life, characters to appear now in one way, now in another. It's this that enabled Toril to give a certain kind of performance of herself to Alex, in part II and part III of "One Another."

For understanding emotions, Goffman's most instructive work, in my view, is his essay "Fun in games," an investigation of the nature of happiness and other emotions.

In life as in drama, people take on and enact roles that are afforded by the interactions they enter. Goffman showed that we can think of each kind of social interaction—in a café, in the home, at school—as like a game. When we enter a game such as tennis or Monopoly, we pass through an invisible membrane into a world that has its own rules, its own traditions, its own history.

In day-to-day life, it's the same. Enacting such roles might include buying a cup of coffee in the café, expressing warmth to your spouse at home, being a student and asking something of a teacher.

For each role, we follow certain outline scripts. Just as in tennis we learn to hit the ball over the net in such a way as to make it difficult for the other player to return, so in a café, we ask politely for the kind of coffee we would like and pay for it. To grab the coffee and leave without paying would attract censure. Each performance we give is viewed by others and ourselves as good or bad in terms of its underlying script, morally worthy or unworthy. Although commentary on one's actions as a café customer may not be frequent, the performance of roles such as spouse or student can give rise to a great deal of commentary by ourselves and others that may include praise, blame, and suggested modifications. Because there are scripts, rules, and customs, the worlds within the invisible membranes that enclose them become moral worlds. They provide the subject matter for much of our conversation.

The essence of Goffman's proposal is that life is social, and that its meanings are jointly constructed by selves and others. The simulations we run in our consciousness, and the models we make of others, derive from our sense of the ways in which we jointly create the meanings in which we are engaged.

Life is not just a matter of whether we give performances within each role that commentators might see as praiseworthy or blameworthy, although such commentaries provide opportunities for many emotions. A central question becomes how engaged we are in each of our roles. We expect to have fun in games, says Goffman, because a game has been constructed specifically to allow us to enter it in a spirit of wholehearted engagement. Usually, we play tennis or Monopoly only if we want to, and because we enjoy getting fully into it. By extension, we can observe that we enjoy our life when we are fully engaged in the roles in which we take part, and we suffer various kinds of distress when we are not.[7]

Orhan Pamuk has proposed the idea that each work of fiction has what he calls a secret center, its real subject, for which we search as readers, and around which the writer has based the story. Pamuk's idea that the center is secret is a very good one, because it points to the fact that really it's the search for it that's important, and the center is different for different readers. For the writer, too, it may be different than it is for readers, and that's because, in writing, the writer, too, has been involved in a search.

For me, "One Another" has a center—I think—somewhere near the issue that Goffman explored in "Fun in games," of asking what it is to be engaged in what one is doing, and of what it is to balance private concerns with those of a relationship. I didn't know this would be the center of my story until I'd gone through many drafts.

I wanted to write a story in which the protagonist was a decent person, but divided in himself. As I was writing, and trying to incorporate various modes and moods that would enable me to discuss the emotions of fiction, I found that Alex was vulnerable to being distracted from himself. Having a clear plan is usually enough to enable one to concentrate wholeheartedly on what one is doing, but not for Alex. Love is usually taken as the state in which one can be most wholehearted, but not for Alex. So without me fully realizing that this is what it would be about, the secret center of the story turned out to be wholeheartedness. Toril is not wholehearted. Sonya is wholehearted. Alex is in between. The tensions between East and West turned out to be an appropriate setting. The story turned out to be about whether Alex is able to be in a wholehearted relationship with Sonya, about whether his experiences might change him. It turned out to be about whether Sonya might be able to recognize what has happened to Alex, and know whether he could be in a wholehearted relationship with her.

THE IDEA OF ROLE

The idea of role,[8] without which social science would now be almost incomprehensible, came before Goffman, but from the same intuition as his. As we go through life, we enter a series of roles: child, student, spouse, worker, parent. In the speech from Shakespeare's *As You Like It*, that starts with "All the world's a stage," Jaques continues: "and one man in his time plays many parts." This insight can be traced even further back. Epictetus, in the first century CE, extending his idea that we can do only what is in our own power, proposed that each of us has a part to play in the world. "It is enough if every man fully discharges the work that is his own."[9]

The simulation that is the conscious theater of the mind reflects the theater of the world. The theater of the mind is more shadowy, more insubstantial, more fragmentary than the outer world of things and people, and also more verbal. The outer world is vividly perceived—seen, heard, and touched—solid, substantial, and complete.[10] However, the inner world is the means by which we can understand the outer world, the means by which we can talk with others about it.

Fiction may be thought of as enabling us mentally to multiply the roles we enter, and to gather to ourselves the extensions of our experience. Just as the playing of hide-and-seek in childhood was important for learning to interact with others, and to understand what they would be thinking and feeling, so fiction enables further extensions of this kind.

In his PhD thesis on the reading of fiction—strikingly called *The Moral Laboratory*—Frank Hakemulder assigned university students to read either a chapter of a novel about the difficult life of an Algerian woman, or an essay on women's rights in Algeria. As compared with those who read the essay, people who read the extract from the novel entered the role of the protagonist and reported that they would be less likely to accept the kinds of roles currently available to women in Algerian society. In another experiment on the same fictional material, Hakemulder found decreased tolerance for current roles of Algerian women among students who were given instructions to think themselves into the situation of the female protagonist of the fictional story, as compared with those who were given instructions to mark the structure of the text with a pencil as they read the story. As the people who engaged with the female protagonist in the fictional story in the study became more like her, they judged the issue of women's rights in Algeria differently.

If, as readers of "One Another," we've been able to enter into the role of Alex or of Sonya or both, we may reflect on what kinds of issues in our own lives we become intransigent about. What do we think we should do? How often, when we are having an argument with a loved one, do we think we are absolutely in the right, and the other is absolutely in the wrong?

PROUST'S WAY

Not far into *Du Côté de Chez Swann*, the first book of his long novel *À la Recherche du Temps Perdu*, Marcel Proust wrote as follows (this translation and others from Proust are mine):

A real person, however profoundly we sympathize with him, is perceived largely by our senses. This means that he remains opaque to us, and offers a dead weight that our perceptions cannot lift. If a misfortune should strike him, it is only in a small part of the total understanding we have of him that we can be moved by this (p. 87).

And lest we think that looking into our own soul is substantially easier, Proust says:

Even more, it is only in a part of the total understanding he has of himself that [the reader] can be moved by himself (p. 87).

This is not just a shortcoming of any particular individual. It is the human condition. We need assistance. Part of this assistance, Proust continues, is literature.

The discovery of the writer of fiction is the idea of replacing those parts that are impenetrable to the mind by an equal quantity of immaterial parts, that is to say parts that our minds can assimilate (p. 87).

Proust goes on to suggest, and indeed to demonstrate in his novel, that one of the functions of literature is to enable us to know other people more intimately than we can generally know them in ordinary life. From this literary knowing, we can become better able to understand people in the ordinary world. At the same time, says Proust, it enables us to know ourselves better.

In reality, when he reads, each person is actually the reader of his own self. The work of the writer is nothing more than

a kind of optical instrument that the writer offers. It allows
the reader to discern that which, without the book, he might
not have been able to see in himself (*Le Temps Retrouvé*,
p. 276)

Although understanding people is among the things we
human beings do best, we are not as good at it as we might be.
The problem lies in the fact that, although another person's eyes
may give us glimpses of that person, they are not windows into
the soul. What others say is another clue, but only a clue. There
is no easy way to know others fully. The best way is through love,
but another way is through fiction.

The emotions of a writer of fiction are no different from
those of other people. The only differences are that the writer
has devoted time and effort into exploring particular emotional
issues, and has learned how to externalize some occasions for
such issues into a particular piece of fiction. Such an externalization is what Lewis Hyde has called a gift that the writer can offer
to a reader.

In Proust's most famous scene—the one with the madeleine
cake—Marcel comes home one day and drinks some herb tea
in which he soaks a piece of cake. Suddenly, he is filled with joy,
like the joy of being in love.[11] Although the taste of tea and cake
summons for him a childhood memory, it's not the memory as
such that brings him joy. It's the sense of experience—which too
often passes one by—being brought together with its meaning.
The idea of bringing together experience and meaning became
the secret center of Proust's novel.

The experience of being able to read and feel and think into
a piece of fiction, although it may sometimes be sad, can also be
profoundly joyful. It can be joyful, I think, because it enables

understanding of our selves to grow and expand, in the way that—as Proust puts it—love can do. This happens, not so much because of the imitation of life by art, but as we build a world in which we are closely involved. It happens when we allow the literary muse of passion to enable our own selves to bring meaning to life in relation to literary selves.

NOTES

Chapter 1 Enjoyment

1. Books of more than one genre were written in medieval times, for instance Boethius's *The Consolation of Philosophy* of 524 was a set of Latin poems that alternated with a sections of prose dialogue. Eight-hundred years later Dante wrote *Vita Nuova*, a set of 31 poems each accompanied by a piece of prose autobiography and a structural analysis of the poem. I have been influenced by David Lodge who has written twin books: The novel *Thinks* about a cognitive scientist working on the problem of consciousness, alongside a nonfiction essay "Consciousness and the Novel." Here, I have put Lodge's two modes between the same covers. The current book also owes something to Italo Calvino's novel *If on a Winter's Night a Traveller*, in which he discusses with readers the very novel they are reading, which is really a set of episodes each written to illustrate a certain kind of fictional effect. It owes something, too, to Marcel Proust's *À la Récherche du Temps Perdu* and W.G. Sebald's books, e.g. *The Rings of Saturn*, which have aspects of essay and fiction. In a book that leans more toward analysis, alternation between pieces of fiction and pieces of discussion has been done best, I think, by Erich Auerbach, in *Mimesis*.
2. The works mentioned in this sentence are William Shakespeare's *Hamlet*, Gustave Flaubert's *Madame Bovary*, and Leo Tolstoy's *Anna Karenina*—which also is the novel that Alex opens on the train, and starts to read the passage in which Anna is on a train, chapter 29, p. 99.

3. Helene Cixous (1974), for instance, warns that whatever might be meant by "character," is not only mistaken, but reductive and repressive. "So long as we do not put aside 'character' and everything that it implies in terms of illusion and complicity with classical reasoning and the appropriating economy that such reasoning supports, we will remain locked up in the treadmill of reproduction" (p. 387).

4. Lynn Hunt's concern is with the way in which fiction contributed to the development of the political idea of human rights. "Human rights grew out of the seedbed sowed by these feelings [empathetic feelings such as are engendered in reading fiction]. Human rights could only flourish when people learned to think of others as their equals, as like them in some fundamental fashion" (p. 58). Her remarks on empathy are from p. 39 of her book, and her citation from Diderot is from her pp. 55–56.

5. *Vertigo* was directed by Alfred Hitchcock, and *Blade Runner* by Ridley Scott.

6. See for instance, Alexander Solzhenitsyn's *The First Circle,* and Joseph Brodsky's *Less Than One.*

7. See, for instance, Suzanne Keen's book *Empathy and the Novel.*

8. Adam Smith did not neglect the literary in his book. As Martha Nussbaum explains in *Poetic Justice,* he proposed that when we think about a character we become judicious spectators, emotionally involved, sympathetic, but also able to make judgments about his or her actions. He thought that the same stance was critical to thinking about justice in society.

9. See Edward Jones & Richard Nisbett, and also Marisa Bortolussi, Peter Dixon, & Paul Sopcak.

10. See Nico Frijda (1993).

11. This method is developed from an idea of Steen Larsen and Uffe Seilman (1988).

12. See Angela Biason's PhD thesis, and for a summary see Oatley (2002).

13. At Angela Biason's PhD oral, the external examiner said that a large American television network had just withdrawn its last teenage soap-opera that had a female protagonist. They were right to do so, because the results we found indicated that boys would be less likely to watch it and that the girls would be equally able to watch soaps with male or female leads. This, in part, is why I chose a male protagonist for "One Another."

14. This lovely phrase about reliving past emotions, used by C.K. Scott Moncrieff in his translation of Marcel Proust's *À la Recherche du Temps Perdu,* is from William Shakespeare's Sonnet 30 (see Helen Vender, 1997) the first eight lines of which are as follows:

When to the sessions of sweet silent thought
I summon up remembrance of things past,

I sigh the lack of many a thing I sought,
And with old woes new wail my dear time's waste;
Then can I drown an eye (unused to flow)
For precious friends hid in death's dateless night,
And weep afresh love's long-since-cancelled woe,
And moan th'expense of many a vanished night.

Chapter 2 The Suspense of Plot

1. It's become fashionable to refer to *plot* as a four-letter word, and imply that it should be replaced by something else. Certainly, in modern, and even postmodern, fiction one wants to engage not just with the what-happens-nextness of plot. However, even the greatest modernist novels are based on a plot as the project and actions of a protagonist. Virginia Woolf's *Mrs Dalloway*, is based on the preparations for and accomplishment of Clarissa Dalloway's party, and Marcel Proust's *À la Recherche du Temps Perdu*, is based on Marcel's plan to write his novel.

2. Jerome Bruner calls the mode of thinking about the workings of the physical world "paradigmatic." The narrative mode of thinking about people as agents starts early in life; see for instance, Charles Fernyhough's fascinating account of his daughter's development, *The Baby in the Mirror*, including the development of her language, which was able to articulate other aspects of her selfhood.

3. In psychology, Fritz Heider and Mary Ann Simmel (1944) showed people a short animated film of two triangles and a circle moving in and around a rectangle. People saw the rectangle as a house, and the triangles and circle as people whom they saw enacting stories such as abandonment by a lover.

4. Another, more emotionally focused and more personal, version of the idea of script was offered by Sylvan Tomkins (1979), who gave the following example. Imagine a girl who, at a young age, is separated from her parents and taken into a hospital where she has to stay for several nights, so that an emergency procedure can be performed. A script—that is to say a sequence of events—is set up as a memory: an incomprehensible separation from parents, the sadness and fear of being alone and of not knowing what would happen, the appearance of a doctor in a white coat and other strangers doing incomprehensible things, the suffering of pain. Subsequently, what can happen is that just one element of this script can set off a reliving of the whole sequence all over again: seeing a man in a white coat can make the girl panic, any threat of separation from parents is met with oppositional tantrums. The traumatic sequence is an example of a negative script, which is stored

in individual memory, and can be triggered by new events that remind one of it. Also on the subject of scripts and how they can suggest emotions, see Oatley (2004).

5. In computer games, which have overtaken movies in the size of their industry and income, players obviously can influence what happens. Peter Vorderer, Sylvia Knobloch, & Holger Schramm (2001) have shown, too, that, if in a TV movie, viewers are able to choose a significant action of one of the characters, for a sizable proportion of them, their engagement in the movie is increased. However, in video games, and in this example of TV interactivity, the insulation from day-to-day life is the same as in fiction.

6. This quotation is from Dolf Zillmann (2000), p. 38. Zillmann has proposed the highly regarded theory, called disposition theory, according to which we acquire a disposition to like characters who behave well in fiction, and to dislike those who behave badly, see also Zillmann (1996).

7. Robert Louis Stevenson (1884/1992): "Life is monstrous, infinite, illogical, abrupt and poignant; a work of art in comparison is neat, finite, self-contained, rational, flowing, and emasculate. Life imposes by brute energy, like inarticulate thunder; art catches the ear, among the far louder noises of experience, like an air artificially made by a discreet musician" (p. 182).

8. This quote is from Noêl Carroll (1997, p. 191).

9. Ronnie de Sousa has thoughtfully discussed the implications of David Hume's reflection that it's far easier to imagine ourselves transported to another world than to imagine ourselves with very different moral values than the ones we hold.

10. Dolf Zillmann (1996) discusses his idea of excitation transfer, and attributes excitation by empathetic distress to the sympathetic division of the autonomic nervous system.

11. As members of the general population, more of the young men who were asked to take part in the study were likely to have been straight rather than gay.

12. For the male interviewer in Donald Dutton and Arthur Aron's (1974) first experiment, 7 out of 20 men accepted the phone number after crossing the high bridge, and 6 out of 20 after crossing the low bridge. Of these men, respectively, 2 and 1 made a phone call to him. Of course, you may say, those who crossed the high bridge—a tourist attraction—had personalities that were more adventurous. Dutton and Aron ruled this out by a second experiment. Men who crossed the high bridge were met by a woman interviewer either immediately after they crossed the bridge or after a 10-minute delay as they walked in the park. Sexual imagery and phone calls from the men to the female interviewer were

more frequent immediately after the men crossed the bridge than after the delay. In a third experiment Dutton and Aron moved to the laboratory. Male participants sat in a room, and just after they sat down another person entered, supposedly another participant in the experiment like themselves. They did not talk to each other. The other person was in fact an accomplice of the experimenters, an attractive woman who sat three feet to one side of the man and a bit in front of him. The experiment was supposedly on the effects of electric shock on learning. Each participant and the accomplice tossed a coin to find whether they would receive a painful or a nonpainful shock (a mere tingle), and each went to a separate cubicle to write about an ambiguous picture of a woman (the same picture that had been used in the interview at the bridges). Participants who had been made more anxious by expecting a painful shock were more attracted to the female accomplice, and had more sexual imagery in response to the ambiguous picture than those who expected the nonpainful shock, and they were more likely to say in a questionnaire that they were attracted to, and would like to kiss, the woman who sat with them (the accomplice).

13. See Nico Tinbergen (1951).

Chapter 3 Falling in Love

1. *Anna Karenina* is a story of Anna's love affair with the dashing Count Vronsky, the beginning of which depends on both Anna and Vronsky being less than fully committed to relationships they were in.

2. Abhinavagupta was one of the principal theorists of *dhvani* and *rasas*. The verse about the traveler is discussed at length by him (see D.H.H. Ingalls et al., 1990 p. 98).

3. The originator of the idea of Rasaboxes was Richard Schechner (2001).

4. Elaine Hatfield was then writing under another name, Elaine Walster. The article to which I refer here is by Elaine Walster & Ellen Berscheid (1971).

5. See Nico Frijda (1988).

6. Within the *rasa*-script of the heroic, *fall* would have a meaning that is completely different from that of the amorous, and prompt ideas of danger or defeat.

7. Here is the Harlequin web site: http://www.eharlequin.com/. According to an encyclopedia article by Tina Gianoulis, http://findarticles.com/p/articles/mi_g1epc/is_tov/ai_2419100567/?tag=content;col1 in 2002 the Harlequin publishing house controlled 85 percent of the romance market worldwide. In 2006 it sold 131 million books. It's still very successful, with 1,300 writers. Gianoulis describes how these books

must be written: "With strict guidelines as to length (exactly 192 pages for 'Harlequin Presents' novels), and content (plots 'should not be too grounded in harsh realities;' writers should avoid such topics as drugs, terrorism, politics, sports, and alcoholic heroes), Harlequin does not allow much room for pesky creativity that could lead to failure. Traditional romance novels all loosely follow the same formula: a young and beautiful heroine with a romantic name such as Selena, Storm, or Ariana, meets a rakishly handsome man, often older and darkly brooding, with a romantic name such as Bolt, Colt, or Holt. They encounter difficulties—perhaps she is unsure for most of the novel whether the man is hero or villain—but by the end they are passionately reconciled. Happy endings are an absolute requirement for the Harlequin Romance." Harlequin was one of the first publishers to realize that, rather than each book being idiosyncratic and distinctive, books could be sold alongside soup and soap flakes in supermarkets. This publishing model was so successful that all publishers have been affected by it.

8. Sherlock Holmes was Arthur Conan Doyle's detective, who appeared in several novels and many short stories, and Hercule Poirot was one of Agatha Christie's detectives. He appeared in many novels, for instance *The Murder of Roger Ackroyd*.

Chapter 4 *Loss and Sadness*

1. Seema Nundy's results appear in her 1996 thesis, and are summarized by Oatley (1996).
2. In this study, not everybody gave reasons for their answers. For those who did, Nundy and I categorized the responses without knowing who was made sad and who was made angry, and we achieved 91 percent agreement between us. The associations between forward chaining and anger, and between backward chaining and sadness, were statistically significant in this study.
3. This interpretation was suggested to me by Patrick Hogan.
4. See also, Mary Beth Oliver and Anne Bartsch (2010).

Chapter 5 *Transformation*

1. For the archaeological findings in this paragraph: the beads were discovered by Abdeljalil Bouzouggar et al. (2007); the flute is discussed by D. Huron (2003), the human burial sites by James Bowler et al. (2003), and the cave paintings by Jean-Marie Chauvet et al. (1996).
2. See Robin Dunbar (2004) and (2009).

3. The word in this fragment of Sappho that is usually translated as "bittersweet" (see, for example, Josephine Balmer's translation, fragment # 2) is *glucopicron,* "sweet-bitter."

4. Paul Harris's book *Work of the Imagination* is the best introduction I know to children's imagination and more recently Alison Gopnik, in *The Philosophical Baby,* has also explored children's abilities to imagine other minds and other worlds.

5. In "One Another," the visit of Alex and Sonya to Poland coincides with the run-up to Polish elections in which the success was established of the Solidarność movement, co-founded by Lech Walesa who would later become Poland's president.

6. In addition, Marc Sestir and Melanie Green (2010) asked viewers either to transport themselves into the narrative: "to focus on the events as if you were inside the movie itself," or instead to "focus on the color scheme used in the movie clip." The instructions to transport themselves into the film did not consistently induce viewers to take on the movie character's traits.

7. Not all fiction necessarily has beneficial effects; indulging too continuously in some kinds of fantasy may distract us from real-world concerns and constraints.

8. See, for instance, William James (1902).

9. See George Brown & Tirril Harris (1987), also Oatley & Djikic (2002).

10. See Bernard Rimé (2009).

Chapter 6 Anger and Retribution

1. See Patrick Hogan (2003).

2. See, for instance, Jean Briggs (1970), who describes an Inuit society that, although it's not without status, does seem to do without anger.

3. This experiment is described by Leonard Berkowitz et al. (1981); a more general account is given by Berkowitz (1993).

4. There are at least three versions of this saying; they are given in a Wikipedia article: http://en.wikipedia.org/wiki/Chekhov's gun

5. The idea that the interpersonal aspect of an emotion is a commitment is due to Michel Aubé (2009).

Chapter 7 Other Minds

1. The two experiments mentioned in this and the previous paragraph are Raymond Mar, Keith Oatley, Jacob Hirsh, Jennifer dela Paz, and Jordan Peterson (2006) and Mar, Oatley, and Peterson (2009).

2. A recent and influential book to make a case for an evolutionary deriva-
   tion of fiction from play is by Brian Boyd (2009).
3. The literature on the possible influence on young people of violence on
   television and in video games is very large. A representative example is
   L. Rowell Huesman (2007).
4. This trait is agreeableness, one of the big-five traits of personality—
   extroversion, neuroticism, agreeableness, conscientiousness, openness—
   which are frequently used in personality assessment, and recently, too,
   have been applied to characters in fiction by Robert McCrea, James
   Gaines, and Marie Wellington (in press).
5. The effects of gender on reading is a perennial issue because, in large
   surveys, it's invariably found that many more women than men read
   literary fiction; in the last large U.S. survey by the National Endowment
   for the Arts (2009), 58 percent of women read a play, poetry, short-
   story, or novel during the previous year, as compared 42 percent of
   men.
6. This research includes that by Angela Biason & Keith Oatley, mentioned
   in Chapter 1.
7. Within my reading, the closest the short story in English comes to offer-
   ing a round character is Gabriel Conroy in James Joyce's "The Dead,"
   but even Gabriel Conroy is not round in the way that some characters
   in novels can become.

Chapter 8 Reflection

1. I introduced this idea in Oatley (1992), and expounded it further in
   1999.
2. Martha Nussbaum has gone on from *The Fragility of Goodness* to argue,
   in *Poetic Justice*, that the kind of thinking and feeling prompted by the
   reading of fiction is essential to justice in society.
3. Silvia Galdi et al. (2008) studied people's conscious thinking and
   subconscious associations about a controversial proposal to enlarge
   a U.S. military base in their city. People were assessed at one point in
   time (time 1) and again a week later (time 2). Conscious beliefs were
   assessed by a 10-item questionnaire on environmental, social, and eco-
   nomic consequences of the proposal. Associations were measured by an
   implicit association test, in which people pressed buttons in response
   to pictures of the military base and evaluative words. People's decisions were measured by them saying whether they were (1) in favor of
   the base's enlargement, (2) undecided, or (3) against the enlargement.
   For the decided people, their conscious thoughts at time 1 were highly

predictive ($p < 0.001$) of their decision at time 2 and also of their automatic associations at time 2 ($p < 0.01$); but these people's automatic associations at time 1 were not predictive of their time 2 decisions. By contrast, among undecided participants, their conscious thoughts at time 1 did not significantly predict their decision at time 2, but their unconscious associations did significantly predict their time 2 decision ($p < 0.05$) and their time 2 conscious beliefs ($p < 0.01$). This study may seem rather complicated. My understanding is that it indicates that our conscious thoughts are affected by processes of which we are not aware and that, rather than conscious thoughts immediately controlling what we decide they can, instead, work over a longer term to affect the structure of our minds, for instance as we think about an issue and discuss it.

4. One possible counterinstance to the idea that human languages lend themselves to a kind of simulation function suggested by Roy Baumeister and E.J. Masicampo is a language group studied by Daniel Everett in South America, the Piraha, in which people live entirely in the here and now, and do not take part in abstract thought or compose stories of their own.

5. James Joyce first used the idea of epiphany as a "sudden spiritual manifestation, whether in the vulgarity of speech or of gesture or in a memorable phase of the mind itself," in *Stephen Hero*, see http://theliterarylink.com/joyce.html

6. This quotation from Scott Fitzgerald, is from Michael Burke, p. 1. In the last part of his book, Burke moves toward the culmination of the reading experience. He gave readers the last few paragraphs of Fitzgerald's *The Great Gatsby*. Of 16 subjects who had read the entire novel, 6 said that the last part did have the effect of prompting an epiphany in them. Among the 20 subjects who read just the closing section of *The Great Gatsby*, only one experienced an epiphany, though several said that if they had read the whole novel they might have done so. Perhaps, as Burke remarks, the influence of the empirical tester and the short passages such testers typically offer readers are not as conducive as we might like to the kinds of questions we want to ask. One person did write about lingering aftereffects: "somehow I am still reading in my mind" (p. 230).

7. In much of life, there seems to be less choice about full engagement than in playing tennis or Monopoly. In life there can be inner conflict. "Do I want to continue this role as employee in this job?" or "Am I doing well enough in my role as student?" We may find we have a certain ability, enact the scripts the ability affords—for instance in roles of employee or student—so that we can give pleasure to others and ourselves.

We may try to follow a set of rules but find that we bungle some action. We try to enact a certain script but find that we don't know how to do things properly. We may take part in an interaction but wish we were elsewhere. Here can occur both satisfying and distressing aspects of our lives, experienced as emotions.

8. The idea of role was proposed first in social science by Ralph Linton.

9. Epictetus, *Enchiridon*, 24: http://www.gutenberg.org/files/10661/10661-h/10661-h.htm

10. Since Hermann von Helmholtz's (1866) work, we know, too, that even the world we see and hear—vivid as it seems—is a construction of our mind, not patterns of excitation of sense organs but a perceived world extended in space of solid objects that can be used or avoided, and people who can be met.

11. Marcel Proust's scene with madeleine cake is this: "And then, mechanically, oppressed by a dispiriting day and the prospect of the next day being miserable too, I carried to my lips a spoonful of the tea with which I had moistened a piece of madeleine cake. At the very instant that the mouthful of tea mixed with cake touched my palate, I trembled, attentive to the extraordinary thing that was happening to me. A delicious pleasure had entered me, isolated, without my having any idea of its cause. It had immediately made life's vicissitudes indifferent, its disasters harmless, its brevity illusory, in the same way that love works by filling me with a precious essence: or, rather, this essence was not in me, it was me. I stopped feeling mediocre, mortal, living a life of contingency. Wherever could it have come from, this powerful joy?" (*Du Côté de Chez Swann*, p. 44, my translation).

BIBLIOGRAPHY

Where I have mentioned an author, to avoid clutter, I have usually omitted giving a date in the text itself. The work to which I refer can be easily found in this list of references.

Aristotle. (1965). *Poetics*. In (T. S. Dorsch., Trans.) *Aristotle, Horace, Longinus: Classical Literary Criticism*. (pp. 29–75). London: Penguin. (Original work published c. 330 BCE).

Aristotle. (1970). *Poetics*. (G. E. Else, Trans.). Ann Arbor, MI: University of Michigan Press. (Original work published c. 330 BCE).

Aubé, M. (2009). Unfolding commitments management: A systemic view of emotions. In J. Valverdu & D. Casacuberta (Eds.), *Handbook of Research on Synthetic Emotions and Sociable Robotics: New Applications in Affective Computing and Artificial Intelligence* (pp. 198–227). Hershey, PA: IGI Global. Online: http://www.igi-global.com/reference/details.asp?ID=34432

Auerbach, E. (1953). *Mimesis: The Representation of Reality in Western Literature* (W. R. Trask, Trans.). Princeton, NJ: Princeton University Press.

Austen, J. (1906). *Pride and Prejudice*. London: Dent. (Original work published 1813)

Averill, J. R. (1982). *Anger and Aggression. An Essay on Emotion*. New York: Springer.

Banks, R. (2001). "Sarah Cole: A type of love story." In R. Banks, *The Angel on the Roof* (pp. 149–175). Toronto: Random House.

Bartsch, A., Vorderer, P., Mangold, R., & Viehoff, R. (2008). Appraisal of emotions in media use: Toward a process model of meta-emotion and emotion regulation. *Media Psychology, 11*, 7–27.

Bartlett, F. C. (1932). *Remembering: A Study in Experimental and Social Psychology*. Cambridge, England: Cambridge University Press.

Baumeister, R. F., & Masicampo, E. J. (2010). Conscious thought is for facilitating social and cultural interactions: How mental simulations serve the animal-culture interface. *Psychological Review, 117*, 945–971.

Bentley, E. C. (1981). *Trent Intervenes*. New York: Dover. (Original work published 1938).

Berkowitz, L. (1993). Towards a general theory of anger and emotional aggression: Implications of a cognitive neo-associationistic perspective for the analysis of anger and other emotions. In R. S. Wyer & T. Srull (Eds.), *Advances in Social Cognition* (Vol. 6, pp. 1-46). Hillsdale, NJ: Erlbaum.

Berkowitz, L., Cochran, S., & Embree, M. (1981). Physical pain and the goal of aversively stimulated aggression. *Journal of Personality and Social Psychology, 40*, 687–700.

Bharata Muni. (1986). *Natyasastra*. (A. Rangacharya, Trans.). Bangalore: IBH Prakashana (Original work published c. 200 BCE).

Biason, A. (1993). *Emotional Responses of High-school Students to Short Stories*. Unpublished doctoral dissertation, University of Toronto, Toronto.

Boetius. (1962). *The Consolation of Philosophy* (R. Green, Trans.). Indianapolis: Bobbs-Merrill (d. 524).

Booth, W. C. (1988). *The Company We Keep: An Ethics of Fiction*. Berkeley, CA: University of California Press.

Bortolussi, M., Dixon, P., & Sopčák, P. (2010). Gender and reading. *Poetics, 38*, 299–318.

Bouzouggar, A., Barton, N., Vanhaeren, M., et al., (2007). 82,000-year-old shell beads from North Africa and implications for the origins of modern human behavior. *Proceedings of the National Academy of Sciences of the USA, 104*, 9964–9969.

Bowlby, J. (1978). *Attachment and Loss, Volume 1: Attachment*. Harmondsworth, England: Penguin). (Original work published London: Hogarth Press, 1969).

Bowler, J. M., et al. (2003). New ages for human occupation and climatic change at Lake Mungo, Australia. *Nature, 421*, 837–840.

Boyd, B. (2009). *On the Origin of Stories*. Cambridge, MA: Harvard University Press.

Briggs, J. L. (1970). *Never in Anger: Portrait of an Eskimo Family*. Cambridge, MA: Harvard University Press.

Brodsky, J. (1987). *Less than One: Selected Essays*. Harmondsworth, England: Penguin.

Brown, D. (2003). *The Da Vinci Code*. New York: Doubleday.

Bruner, J. (1986). *Actual Minds, Possible Worlds*. Cambridge, MA: Harvard University Press.

Burke, M. (2011). *Literary Reading, Cognition and Emotion: An Exploration of the Oceanic Mind*. London: Routledge.

Burns, E. (Director). (1995). *The Brothers McMullen* (Film). USA.

Cadieux, K. V. (2008). Intractable characters as personality extensions. (Online). *http://www.onfiction.ca/2008/09/intractable-characters-as-personality.html*

Calvino, I. (1981). *If on a Winter's Night a Traveller* (W. Weaver, Trans.). New York: Harcourt Brace Jovanovich.

Cameron, J. (Director). (2009). *Avatar.* (Film). USA.

Carroll, N. (1997). Art, narrative, and emotion. In M. Hjort & S. Laver (Eds.), *Emotion and the Arts* (pp. 190–211). Oxford: Oxford University Press.

Carroll, N. (2007). Narrative closure. *Philosophical Studies, 135,* 1–15.

Chandler, R. (1939). *The Big Sleep.* New York: Knopf.

Chauvet, J.-M., Deschamps, E. B., & Hillaire, C. (1996). *Dawn of Art: The Chauvet Cave.* New York: Abrams.

Chekhov, A. (1990). "The lady with the toy dog" (S. S. Koteliansky & G. Cannan, Trans.) *Anton Chekhov: Five Great Short Stories* (pp. 81–94). New York: Dover. (Original work published 1899).

Chopin, K. (2000). "The dream of an hour." In P. Knights (Ed.), *Kate Chopin: The Awakening and Other Stories* (pp. 259–261). Oxford: Oxford University Press (original work published 1894).

Christie, A. (1926). *The Murder of Roger Ackroyd.* London: Collins.

Cixous, H. (1974). The character of "character." *New Literary History, 5,* 383–402.

Curtiz, M. (Director). (1942). *Casablanca* (Film). USA.

Dante Alighieri. (1995). *La Vita Nuova* (Trans. Dino Cervigni & Edward Vasta). Notre Dame, IN: University of Notre Dame Press (Original composed between 1292 and 1295).

Derrick, J., Gabriel, S., & Hugenberg, K. (2009). Social surrogacy: How favored television programs provide the experience of belonging. *Journal of Experimental Social Psychology, 45,* 352–362.

De Sousa, R. (2010). The mind's Bermuda Triangle: Philosophy of emotions and empirical science. In P. Goldie (Ed.), *Oxford Companion to Philosophy of Emotions* (pp. 95–117). Oxford: Oxford University Press.

Djikic, M., Oatley, K., & Peterson, J. (2006). The bitter-sweet labor of emoting: The linguistic comparison of writers and physicists. *Creativity Research Journal, 18,* 191–197.

Djikic, M., Oatley, K., Zoeterman, S., & Peterson, J. (2009). On being moved by art: How reading fiction transforms the self. *Creativity Research Journal, 21,* 24–29.

Djikic, M., Oatley, K., Zoeterman, S., & Peterson, J. B. (2009). Defenceless against art? Impact of reading fiction on emotion in avoidantly attached individuals. *Journal of Research in Personality, 43,* 14–17.

Dostoyevsky, F. (1993). *Crime and Punishment* (R. Pevear & L. Volokhonsky, Trans.). New York: Vintage (Original work published 1866).

Doyle, A. C. (1981). *The Complete Adventures of Sherlock Holmes*. London: Penguin.

Dunbar, R. I. M. (2004). *The Human Story: A New History of Mankind's Evolution*. London: Faber.

Dunbar, R. I. M. (2009). Why only humans have language. In R. Botha & C. Knight (Eds.), *The Prehistory of Language* (pp. 12–35). Oxford: Oxford University Press.

Dutton, D. G., & Aron, A. P. (1974). Some evidence for heightened sexual attraction under conditions of high anxiety. *Journal of Personality and Social Psychology, 30,* 510–517.

Eliot, G. (1871–1872). *Middlemarch: A Study of Provincial Life* (Reprinted, Penguin, 1965. ed.). Edinburgh, Scotland: Blackwood.

Eliot, T. S. (1919). *Hamlet*. In J. Hayward (Ed.), *T.S. Eliot: Selected Prose* (pp. 104–109). Harmondsworth, England: Penguin.

Everett, D. L. (2005). Cultural constraints on grammar and cognition in Pirahã: Another look at the design features of human language. *Current Anthropology, 46,* 621–646.

Fernyhough, C. (2008). *The Baby in the Mirror: A Child's World from Birth to Three*. London: Granta.

Fitzgerald, F. S. (1950). *The Great Gatsby*. Harmondsworth, England: Penguin. (Original work published 1926).

Flaubert, G. (1857). *Madame Bovary*. (M. Marmur, Trans.). New York: New American Library.

Forster, E. M. (1924). *A Passage to India*. London: Edward Arnold.

Forster, E. M. (1927). *Aspects of the Novel*. London: Edward Arnold.

Freud, S. (1975). *The Psychopathology of Everyday Life. The Pelican Freud Library, Vol. 5.* (Eds. J. Strachey, A. Richards, & A. Tyson) (A. Tyson, Trans.). London: Penguin. (Original work published 1901).

Freud, S. (1985). Psychopathic characters on the stage. In A. Dickson (Ed.), *Pelican Freud Library, 14: Art and Literature* (pp. 119–127). London: Penguin. (Original work published 1905–1906).

Freud, S. (1985). Creative writers and day-dreaming. In A. Dickson (Ed.), *Pelican Freud Library, 14: Art and Literature* (pp. 130–141). London: Penguin. (Original work published 1908).

Frijda, N. H. (1988). The laws of emotion. *American Psychologist, 43,* 349–358.

Frijda, N. H. (1993). The place of appraisal in emotion. *Cognition and Emotion, 7,* 357–387.

Galdi, S., Arcuri, L., & Gawronsowski, B. (2008). Automatic mental associations predict future choices of undecided decision-makers. *Science, 321,* 1100–1102.

Gardner, W. L., & Knowles, M., L. (2008). Love makes you real: Favorite television characters are perceived as "real" in a social facilitation paradigm. *Social Cognition, 26,* 156–168.

Gerrig, R. J. (1993). *Experiencing Narrative Worlds: On the Psychological Activities of Reading.* New Haven, CT: Yale University Press.

Goffman, E. (1959). *The Presentation of Self in Everyday Life.* New York: Doubleday.

Goffman, E. (1961). Fun in games. In *Encounters: Two Studies in the Sociology of Interaction* (pp. 15–81). Indianapolis, IN: Bobbs-Merrill.

Gopnik, A. (2009). *The Philosophical Baby: What Children's Minds Tell us About Truth, Love, and the Meaning of Life.* New York: Farrar, Straus and Giroux.

Gopnik, A., & Astington, J. W. (1988). Children's understanding of representational change and its relation to their understanding of false belief and the appearance-reality distinction. *Child Development, 58,* 26–37.

Haidt, J. (2003). Elevation and the positive psychology of morality. In C. L. M. Keyes & J. Haidt (Eds.), *Flourishing: Positive Psychology and the Life Well-lived* (pp. 275–289). Washington, DC: American Psychological Association.

Hakemulder, F. (2000). *The Moral Laboratory: Experiments Examining the Effects of Reading Literature on Social Perception and Moral Self-concept.* Amsterdam, Netherlands: Benjamins.

Halliwell, S. (2002). *The Aesthetics of Mimesis: Ancient Texts and Modern Problems.* Princeton, NJ: Princeton University Press.

Hammett, D. (1930). *The Maltese Falcon.* New York: Knopf.

Harris, P. L. (2000). *The Work of the Imagination.* Oxford: Blackwell.

Hatfield, E., & Rapson, R. L. (2000). *Rosie.* Pittsburgh, PA: SterlingHouse.

Heider, F., & Simmel, M. (1944). An experimental study of apparent behavior. *American Journal of Psychology, 57,* 243–259.

Helmholtz, H. von (1962). *Treatise on Physiological Optics, Vol 3* (J. P. C. Southall, Trans.). New York: Dover. (Original work published 1866).

Hitchcock, A. (Director). (1958). *Vertigo* (Film). USA.

Hogan, P. C. (2003). *The Mind and its Stories: Narrative Universals and Human Emotion.* Cambridge, England: Cambridge University Press.

Homer (1987). *The Iliad* (M. Hammond, Ed. and Trans.). Harmondsworth, England: Penguin (Original work devised 850 BCE).

Huesmann, L. R. (2007). The impact of electronic media violence: Scientific theory and research. *Journal of Adolescent Health, 41 (suppl.),* S6–S13.

Hume, D. (1965). Of the standard of taste. In J. W. Lenz (Ed.), *Of the Standard of Taste and Other Essays.* Indianapolis, IN: Bobbs Merrill.

Hunt, L. (2007). *Inventing Human Rights.* New York: Norton.

Huron, D. (2003). Is music an evolutionary adaptation? In I. Peretz & R. Zatorre (Eds.), *The Cognitive Neuroscience of Music* (pp. 57–75). Oxford: Oxford University Press.

Hyde, L. (1983). *The Gift: Imagination and the Erotic Life of Property.* New York: Vintage.

Ingalls, D. H. H., Masson, J. M., & Patwardhan, M. V. (1990). *The Dhvanyaloka of Anandavardana with the Locana of Abhinavagupta.* Cambridge, MA.: Harvard University Press.

Isen, A. (1987). Positive affect, cognitive processes, and social behavior. In L. Berkowitz (Ed.), *Advances in Experimental Social Psychology* (pp. 203–253). San Diego: Academic Press.

James, W. (1982). *The Varieties of Religious Experience.* New York: Viking Penguin (Original work published 1902).

Johnson, J. A., Carroll, J., Gottschall, J., & Kruger, D. (2011). Portrayal of personality in Victorian novels reflects modern research finding but amplifies the significance of agreeableness. *Journal of Research in Personality, 45,* 50–58.

Jones, E. E., & Nisbett, R. E. (1971). *The Actor and the Observer: Divergent Perceptions of the Causes of Behavior.* New York: General Learning Press.

Joyce, J. (1976). The dead. In J. Joyce, *Dubliners.* London: Penguin. (Original work published 1914).

Keen, S. (2007). *Empathy and the Novel.* New York: Oxford University Press.

Kermode, F. (1966). *The Sense of an Ending: Studies in the Theory of Fiction.* Oxford: Oxford University Press.

Larsen, S. F., & Seilman, U. (1988). Personal meanings while reading literature. *Text, 8,* 411–429.

Larsson, S. (2008). *The Girl with the Dragon Tattoo* (R. Keeland, Trans.). New York: Vintage.

Leder, M. (Director). (2000). *Pay it Forward* (Film). USA.

Libet, B. (1985). Unconscious cerebral initiative and the role of conscious will in voluntary action. *Behavioral and Brain Sciences, 8,* 529–566.

Linton, R. (1936). *The Study of Man.* New York: Appleton-Century-Crofts.

Lodge, D. (2001). *Thinks.* London: Secker & Warburg.

Lodge, D. (2002). Consciousness and the novel. In D. Lodge (Ed.), *Consciousness and the Novel* (pp. 1–91). Cambridge, MA: Harvard University Press.

Mar, R. A. (2007). *Simulation-Based Theories of Narrative Comprehension: Evidence and Implications.* Doctoral dissertation. University of Toronto, Toronto.

Mar, R. A., Oatley, K., Hirsh, J., dela Paz, J., & Peterson, J. B. (2006). Bookworms versus nerds: Exposure to fiction versus non-fiction, divergent associations with social ability, and the simulation of fictional social worlds. *Journal of Research in Personality, 40,* 694–712.

Mar, R. A., Oatley, K., & Peterson, J. B. (2009). Exploring the link between reading fiction and empathy: Ruling out individual differences and examining outcomes. *Communications The European Journal of Communication, 34,* 407–428.

Mar, R. A., Tackett, J. L., & Moore, C. (2010). Exposure to media and theory-of-mind development in preschoolers. *Cognitive Development, 25,* 69–78.

McCrea, R. R., Gaines, J. F., & Wellington, M. A. (2012, in press). The five-factor model in fact and fiction. In H. A. Tennen & J. M. Suls (Eds.), *Handbook of Psychology, Vol. V. Personality and Social Psychology*. Hoboken, NJ: Wiley.

McCullers, C. (1963). "Sucker." *Saturday Evening Post*.

Mithen, S. (1996). *The Prehistory of the Mind: The Cognitive Origins of Art and Science*. London: Thames and Hudson.

Munro, A. (1968). "Red dress." In *Dance of the Happy Shades* (pp. 147–160). Toronto: McGraw-Hill.

National Endowment for the Arts. (2009). *Reading on the Rise: A New Chapter in American Literacy* (No. 46). Washington, DC: National Endowment for the Arts.

Nïn, A. (1977). *Delta of Venus*. New York: Harcourt Brace Jovanovich.

Nisbett, R. E., & Wilson, T. D. (1977). Telling more than we can know: Verbal reports on mental processes. *Psychological Review, 84*, 231–259.

Nundy, S. (1996). *Effects of Emotion on Human Inference*. Unpublished doctoral dissertation. University of Toronto, Toronto.

Nussbaum, M. C. (1986). *The Fragility of Goodness: Luck and Ethics in Greek Tragedy and Philosophy*. Cambridge, England: Cambridge University Press.

Nussbaum, M. C. (1995). *Poetic Justice: The Literary Imagination and Public Life*. Boston: Beacon.

Oatley, K. (1992). *Best Laid Schemes: The Psychology of Emotions*. New York: Cambridge University Press.

Oatley, K. (1993). *The Case of Emily V.* London: Secker & Warburg.

Oatley, K. (1996). Inference in narrative and science. In D. R. Olson & N. Torrance (Eds.), *Modes of Thought* (pp. 123-140). New York: Cambridge University Press.

Oatley, K. (1999). Why fiction may be twice as true as fact: Fiction as cognitive and emotional simulation. *Review of General Psychology, 3*, 101–117.

Oatley, K. (2002). Emotions and the story worlds of fiction. In M. C. Green, J. J. Strange & T. C. Brock (Eds.), *Narrative Impact: Social and Cognitive Foundations* (pp. 39–69). Mahwah, NJ: Erlbaum.

Oatley, K. (2004). Scripts, transformations, and suggestiveness, of emotions in Shakespeare and Chekhov. *Review of General Psychology, 8*, 323–340.

O'Connor, F. (2004). *The Lonely Voice*. New York: Melville House. (Original work published by World Publishing, 1963).

Oliver, M. B. (2008). Tender affective states as predictors of entertainment preference. *Journal of Communication, 58*, 40–61.

Oliver, M. B., & Bartsch, A. (2010). Appreciation as audience response: Exploring entertainment gratifications beyond hedonism. *Human Communication Research, 36*, 53–81.

Pamuk, O. (2010). *The Naive and the Sentimental Novelist* (N. Dikbas, Trans.). Cambridge, MA: Harvard University Press.

Panksepp, J. (2005). Affective consciousness: Core emotional feelings in animals and humans. *Consciousness and Cognition, 14,* 30–80.

Proust, M. (1983). *À la Recherche du Temps Perdu (Remembrance of Things Past)* (C. K. Scott-Moncrieff, T. Kilmartin & A. Mayer, Trans.). London: Penguin (Original work published 1913–1927).

Proust, M. (1987). *Du Côté de Chez Swann.* Paris: Gallimard. (Original work published 1913).

Proust, M. (1954). *Le Temps Retrouvé.* Paris: Gallimard. (Original work published 1927).

Radway, J. A. (1984). *Reading the Romance: Women, Patriarchy, and Popular Literature.* Chapel Hill, NC: University of North Carolina Press.

Ransome, A. (1930). *Swallows and Amazons.* London: Cape.

Richardson, S. (2001). *Pamela.* Oxford: Oxford University Press (Original work published 1740).

Rimé, B. (2009). Emotion elicits social sharing of emotion: Theory and empirical review. *Emotion Review, 1,* 60–85.

Rowling, J. K. (1997). *Harry Potter and the Philosopher's Stone.* London: Bloomsbury.

Royzman, E. B., & Rozin, P. (2006). Limits of symhedonia: The differential role of prior emotional attachment in sympathy and sympathetic joy. *Emotion, 6,* 82–93.

Sappho. (1993). *Poems and Fragments* (J. Balmer, Trans.). New York: Carol Publishing Group (Original work circa 580 BCE).

Schank, R., & Abelson, R. (1977). *Scripts, Plans, Goals and Understanding: An Inquiry into Human Knowledge Structures.* Hillsdale, NJ: Erlbaum.

Schechner, R. (2001). Rasaesthetics. *The Drama Review, 43,* 27–50.

Scheff, T. J. (1979). *Catharsis in Healing, Ritual, and Drama.* Berkeley, CA: University of California Press.

Scheff, T., & Retzinger, S. (2001). *Emotions and Violence: Shame and Rage in Destructive Conflicts.* Lincoln, NE: iUniverse.

Schlesinger, J. (Director). (1963). *Billy Liar* (Film). UK.

Schramm, H., & Wirth, W. (2010). Exploring the paradox of sad-film enjoyment: The role of multiple appraisals and meta-appraisals. *Poetics, 38,* 319–335.

Scott, R. (Director). (1982). *Blade Runner* (Film). USA.

Sebald, W. G. (1998). *The Rings of Saturn* (M. Hulse, Trans.). London: Harvill Press.

Sestir, M., & Green, M. C. (2010). You are who you watch: Identification and transportation effects on temporary self-concept. *Social Influence, 5,* 272–288.

Shakespeare, W. (1995). *A Midsummer Night's Dream*. Oxford: Oxford University Press (Original work published 1600).

Shakespeare, W. (1993). *As You Like It (Ed. A. Brissenden)*. Oxford: Oxford University Press. (Original work published 1623).

Shakespeare, W. (1981). *Hamlet* (H. Jenkins, Ed.). London: Methuen. (Original work published 1600).

Shakespeare, W. (1987). *The Tempest* (S. Orgel, Ed). Oxford: Oxford University Press. (Original work published 1623).

Shakespeare, W. (1997). *Richard III*, in *The Norton Shakespeare* (S. Greenblatt, Ed.). (pp. 505–600). New York: Norton. (Original work published 1623).

Shakespeare, W. (2000). *Romeo and Juliet*. (J. Levinson, Ed.) Oxford: Oxford University Press. (Original work published 1599).

Smith, A. (1976). *The Theory of Moral Sentiments*. Oxford: Oxford University Press (Original work published 1759).

Solzhenitsyn, A. (1968). *The First Circle* (M. Guybon, Trans.). London: Collins.

Sternberg, R. J. (1998). *Love Is a Story*. New York: Oxford University Press.

Stevenson, R. L. (1884). A humble remonstrance. *Longman's Magazine, December*, Reprinted in *R. L. Stevenson Essays and Poems* (1992) (C. Harman, Ed.) London: Dent Everyman's Library (pp. 1179–1188).

Stevenson, R. L. (1979). The ebb tide. In *Dr Jekyll and Mr Hyde, and Other Stories* (J. Calder, Ed.) (pp. 171–301). London: Penguin (Original work published 1893).

Stillwell, A. M., Baumeister, R. F., & Del Priore, R. E. (2008). We are all victims here: Towards a psychology of revenge. *Basic and Applied Social Psychology, 30*, 253–263.

Tal-Or, N., & Cohen, J. (2010). Understanding audience involvement: Conceptualizing and manipulating identification. *Poetics, 38*, 402–418.

Tan, E., & Frijda, N. H. (1999). Sentiment in film viewing. In C. Plantinga & G. M. Smith (Eds.), *Passionate Views: Film, Cognition, and Emotion* (pp. 48–64). Baltimore, MD: Johns Hopkins University Press.

Taylor, M., Hodges, S., & Kohányi, A. (2002–2003). The illusion of independent agency: Do adult fiction writers experience their characters as having minds of their own? *Imagination, Cognition, and Personality, 22*, 361–380.

Tinbergen, N. (1951). *The Study of Instinct*. Oxford: Oxford University Press.

Tolstoy, L. (2007). *War and Peace* (R. Pevear & L. Volokonsky, Trans.). New York: Knopf (Original work published 1869).

Tolstoy, L. (2000). *Anna Karenina* (R. Pevear & L. Volokonsky, Trans.). London: Penguin (Original work published 1877).

Tolstoy, L. (2005). Strider (*Kholstomer*). In R. Wilks & P. Foore (Eds.), *Leo Tolstoy: Master and Man, and Other Stories* (pp. 67–107). London: Penguin (Original work published 1885).

Tomasello, M. (2008). *Origins of Human Communication*. Cambridge, MA: MIT Press.

Tomkins, S. S. (1979). Script theory: Differential magnification of affects. In H. E. Howe & R. A. Dienstbier (Eds.), *Nebraska Symposium on Motivation, 1978:* Vol. 26 (pp. 201–236). Lincoln, NA: University of Nebraska Press.

Trabasso, T., & Chung, J. (January 23, 2004). *Empathy: Tracking Characters and Monitoring Their Concerns in Film.* Paper presented at the Winter Text Conference, Jackson Hole, WY.

Vendler, H. (1997). *The Art of Shakespeare's Sonnets*. Cambridge, MA: Harvard University Press.

Vivanco, L., & Kramer, K. (2010). There are six bodies in this relationship: An anthropological approach to the romance genre. *Journal of Popular Romance Studies, 1.* Online 4 August, at http://www.jprstudies.org

Vorderer, P., & Knobloch, S. (2000). Conflict and suspense in drama. In D. Zillmann & P. Vorderer (Eds.), *Media Entertainment: The Psychology of its Appeal* (pp. 59–72). Mahwah, NJ: Erlbaum.

Vorderer, P., Knobloch, S. & Schramm, H. (2001). Does entertainment suffer from interactivity? The impact of watching an interactive TV movie on viewers' experience of entertainment. *Media Psychology, 3,* 343–363.

Walster, E., & Berscheid, E. (1971). Adrenaline makes the heart grow fonder. *Psychology Today, 5*(1), 47–50.

Weber, R., Tamborini, R., Lee, H. E., & Stipp, H. (2008). Soap opera exposure and enjoyment: A longitudinal test of disposition theory. *Media Psychology, 11,* 462–487.

Williams, M. (1922). *The Velveteen Rabbit*. New York: Avon.

Wimmer, H., & Perner, J. (1983). Beliefs about beliefs: Representation and constraining function of wrong beliefs in young children's understanding of deception. *Cognition, 13,* 103–128.

Woolf, V. (1925). *Mrs Dalloway*. London: Hogarth Press.

Zillmann, D. (1994). Mechanisms of emotional involvement with drama. *Poetics, 23,* 33–51.

Zillmann, D. (1996). The psychology of suspense in dramatic exposition. In P. Vorderer, H. J. Wulff & M. Friedrichsen (Eds.), *Suspense: Conceptualizations, Theoretical Analyses, and Empirical Explorations* (pp. 199–231). Mahwah, NJ: Erlbaum.

Zillmann, D. (2000). Humor and comedy. In D. Zillmann & P. Vorderer (Eds.), *Media Entertainment: The Psychology of its Appeal* (pp. 37–57). Mahwah, NJ: Erlbaum.

Zunshine, L. (2006). *Why We Read Fiction: Theory of Mind and the Novel.* Columbus, OH: Ohio State University Press.

NAME INDEX

Abelson, Robert, 46
Abhinavagupta, 70–71, 193
Ackroyd, Roger, 53
Aristotle, 33–34, 44, 121, 142, 172–174
Aron, Arthur, 58, 192–193
Astington, Janet, 156
Aubé, Michel, 195
Auerbach, Erich, 189
Austen, Jane, 77–78, 155
Averill, James, 138–139
Aziz, Dr., 168

Banks, Russell, 93–96
Bartlett, Frederic, 103
Bartsch, Anne, 170
Baumeister, Roy, 176–178, 197
Beethoven, Ludwig van, 102
Bennet, Elizabeth, 77–78, 155
Bentley, E. C., 119
Bergman, Ingrid, 96, 166
Berkowitz, Leonard, 135–136
Biason, Angela, 32
Boethius, 189
Bogart, Humphrey, 96
Booth, Wayne, 162
Bortolussi, Marisa, 167
Bouzouggar, Abdeljalil, 194
Bovary, Emma, 16–17
Bowlby, John, 97
Bowler, James, 194

Briggs, Jean, 195
Brodsky, Joseph, 24
Brooke, Dorothea, 166, 168–169
Brown, Dan, 80
Bruner, Jerome, 23, 45, 191
Burke, Michael, 179–181, 197
Burns, Edward, 55

Cadieux, Valentine, 28
Calvino, Italo, 189
Cameron, James, 54–55
Carroll, Noël, 52–53
Cassio, 160
Chandler, Raymond, 92
Chauvet, Jean-Marie, 194
Chekhov, Anton, 122–124, 137
Chopin, Kate, 100
Christie, Agatha, 53, 164, 194
Christie, Julie, 164
Chung, Jennifer, 22, 25, 49, 56
Cixous, Helene, 190
Cohen, Jonathan, 55
Cole, Sarah, 93–96
Conroy, Gabriel, 196
Curtiz, Michael, 96

Dalloway, Clarissa, 191
Dante, 189
Darcy, Fitzwilliam, 77–78, 155
Derrick, Jaye, 163

SUBJECT INDEX